African Americans and US Popular Culture

African Americans have made a unique contribution to the richness and diversity of US popular culture. Rooted in African society and traditions, black slaves in America created a dynamic culture which keeps on evolving. Present-day Hip Hop and Rap music are shaped by the historical experience of slavery and the ongoing will to oppose oppression and racism.

This volume is an authoritative introduction to the history of African Americans in US popular culture, examining its development from the early nineteenth century to the present. Kevern Verney examines the role and significance of race in all major forms of popular culture, including sport, film, television, radio and music. He also looks at how Hollywood and the entertainment industry have encouraged racism through misrepresentations and caricatured images of African Americans.

Kevern Verney is a Senior Lecturer in American History at Edge Hill College of Higher Education. He is the author of *Black Civil Rights in America* (Routledge 2000) and *The Art of the Possible: Booker T. Washington and Black Leadership in the United States, 1881–1925* (Routledge 2001).

INTRODUCTIONS TO HISTORY

Edited by David Birmingham

This series of introductions to widely studied and newer areas of the undergraduate history curriculum provides short, clear, self-contained and incisive guides for the student reader.

Introductions to History

Series Editor: David Birmingham
Professor of Modern History, University of Kent at Canterbury

A series initiated by members of the School of History at the University of Kent at Canterbury

African Americans and US Popular Culture

Kevern Verney

Routledge
Taylor & Francis Group

LONDON AND NEW YORK

First published 2003
by Routledge
11 New Fetter Lane, London EC4P 4EE

Simultaneously published in the USA and Canada
by Routledge
29 West 35th Street, New York, NY 10001

Routledge is an imprint of the Taylor & Francis Group

© 2003 Kevern Verney

Typeset in Sabon and Gill Sans by Wearset Ltd, Boldon, Tyne and Wear
Printed and bound in Great Britain by TJ International Ltd, Padstow,
Cornwall

British Library Cataloguing in Publication Data
A catalogue record for this book is available from the British Library

Library of Congress Cataloging in Publication Data
Verney, Kevern, 1960–
    African Americans and US popular culture / Kevern Verney.
        p. cm.
Includes bibliographical references and index.
    1. African Americans in popular culture. 2. African Americans—Race
identity. 3. African Americans—Intellectual life. 4. Racism in
popular culture—United States. 5. United States—Race relations. 6.
Popular culture—United States—History. 7. United
States—Civilization—African American influences. I. Title.
    E185.625.V47 2003
    305.896'083—dc21
                                                              2003001026

ISBN 0–415–27527–X (hbk)
ISBN 0–415–27528–8 (pbk)

Contents

Preface

Prior to the 1970s popular culture received comparatively little attention from historians. In recent years this situation has changed. Historians now recognize the importance of popular culture in understanding the past. It provides insight into how, and why, public opinion viewed issues in a particular way. Moreover, it gives a voice to groups, like African Americans, who are under-represented in written records because of their oppressed condition and the limited educational opportunities afforded them.

For these reasons I provided brief coverage of the relationship between popular culture and racial issues in *Black Civil Rights in America*, my first publication for the Routledge Introductions to History series. *African Americans and US Popular Culture* serves as a companion volume examining this topic in greater detail. The chronological periods covered in each chapter correspond with those in the earlier work.

Discussion is focused on a number of key issues, specifically:

- the persistent negative stereotyping of African Americans in popular culture, and the impact this had on the racial perceptions of both black and white Americans;
- the extent to which, over time, popular culture has responded to political, social and economic change;
- the role of popular culture in holding back or facilitating change in US race relations;
- the recurring historical paradox that whilst white Americans have frequently recognized black cultural achievement, African Americans themselves continued to be perceived as socially and racially inferior;

- the enormous, and continuing, contribution made by African Americans to US popular culture.

An inevitable dilemma in any work on popular culture is the question of what subject matter to include, and what to omit. This work is focused primarily on film, music, radio, sport and television. Other areas, like advertising, dance, fashion, literature and oral culture, are discussed, but these constitute secondary themes.

The achievements of African American writers, like James Baldwin and Toni Morrison, and painters, such as Henry Ossawa Tanner, are not considered. Although they have made a major contribution to American culture through their work, it generally has not reached the mass audiences of film and television.

Religion is also omitted. The Church has enormous impact on the lives of black and white Americans, but its role in society transcends that of popular culture. It embodies deep spiritual values that, to believers, represent the revelation of divine truth. To consider religion alongside film, sport and television, de-contextualized from this deeper philosophical meaning, would be to secularize the sacred.

Emancipation and segregation

Modern representations of African Americans in US popular culture begin with the emergence of blackface minstrelsy in 1830–2. The practice of white actors appearing in burnt-cork make-up can be traced back to Elizabethan England, and comic black characters appeared periodically in the American theatre as early as the 1780s. The minstrelsy of the 1830s, however, constituted a clear departure from what had gone before. Minstrel shows marked the first systematic portrayal of African American culture on the American stage with most, if not all, of the performers appearing in blackface.

The principal inspiration in the creation of minstrelsy was the white entertainer Thomas Dartmouth Rice. Living in Kentucky in the late 1820s, Rice reputedly witnessed the performance of an unusual song and dance by an elderly, disabled slave. Mimicking and exaggerating what he had seen, Rice developed a comic musical routine, 'Jumpin' Jim Crow', to entertain local white audiences. The act was an immediate hit. Between 1832 and 1836 Rice played to packed audiences in towns and cities across the northern United States. Domestic triumph was followed by a successful tour of England, Scotland and Ireland that also included a brief visit to Paris.

At the same time that Rice began his rise to fame another blackface performer, George Washington Dixon, began to attract attention. In 1829 Dixon received popular acclaim for his performance of the song 'Coal Black Rose' in burnt-cork make-up at the Bowery theatre in New York. By 1834 Dixon had developed his own minstrel routine performing 'Zip Coon' songs. In contrast to the character of the slow-witted rural slave, represented by Jim Crow, Zip Coon was a pretentious dandy who, although grossly ignorant, was hopelessly inflated with a sense of self-importance. The Jim Crow and Zip Coon caricatures continued as recurring images of African Americans in US popular culture until at least the mid-twentieth century, and arguably beyond.

Dan Emmett, Edwin Christy and Stephen Foster were other leading influences in the early development of minstrelsy. In 1843 Emmett organized the first blackface quartet in New York and thereafter devoted the rest of his career to minstrelsy. The same year Christy formed his own minstrel troupe, 'Christy's Plantation Minstrels'. Foster, a songwriter, made a living by writing numbers for minstrel shows.

The careers of Emmett, Christy and Foster reflect the fact that in the early 1840s minstrel acts developed from being one-man performances to larger-scale entertainments with a cast made up of a variety of characters. No longer brief routines, minstrel shows now took the form of full-length productions.

Typically, the show comprised three parts. They began with a performance of songs and revels by predominantly blackface urban dandies in the Zip Coon mould. A middle section introduced blackface novelty acts, such as comic monologues or drag acts. A final section comprised song and dance numbers performed within the context of a simple narrative storyline, typically in the setting of a southern plantation populated by happy blackface slaves. Despite such imagery, prior to the Civil War the popularity of minstrelsy was confined almost exclusively to the North and Mid-west. In the 1850s the performance of minstrel shows was even made unlawful in some southern cities.

The artistic merit and social significance of minstrelsy have been issues of controversy since its early beginnings. Novelist Mark Twain hailed minstrelsy as a uniquely American form of entertainment. It can also be seen as marking the first public recognition of African American culture by whites, albeit in a grossly distorted form.

Modern historians, like Annemarie Bean, Eric Lott, and William Mahon, have highlighted the complexity of social meaning in minstrelsy. Looking behind the blackface mask, minstrelsy can be valued as an expression of white working-class culture. The comic guise of minstrel performers enabled them to lampoon leading politicians and other authority figures without fear of retribution. From this perspective minstrelsy was not just entertainment, it was also a form of popular social criticism, played before audiences that were predominantly young, male and working class.

Less positively, blackface minstrels targeted women's rights campaigners and minority ethnic groups, like the Germans and Irish, reinforcing negative stereotypes of them. Deriding immigrants as ignorant amused the native white American audiences and at the same time reinforced feelings of ethnic superiority. It calmed working-class anxieties over immigrant labour as a source of competition in the job market. Similarly, the caricaturing of women's rights campaigners, by physically comic and overassertive blackface performers in drag, soothed sensitive male egos over the threat they posed to established gender roles.

Significantly, this occurred at a time when women's suffrage and immigration were both issues of public concern. In 1848 the Seneca Falls Convention in New York marked the emergence of a concerted women's suffrage movement. Fears over rising levels of immigration in the 1840s prompted the formation of nativist or anti-immigrant organizations like the secret society the 'Know Nothings'.

Minstrelsy was complex in meaning. Nonetheless, it is difficult to avoid the conclusion that the central feature of the genre was the appropriation of African American culture by white entertainers in a way that maximized negative stereotypes. Frederick Douglass, an escaped slave, and the leading black abolitionist of his day, found minstrel shows deeply offensive. Blackface performers were 'the filthy scum of white society' who had 'stolen from us a complexion denied to them by nature' in order to 'make money and pander to the corrupt taste of their white fellow citizens'.

The growth of the minstrel phenomenon in the early 1830s coincided almost exactly with the emergence of radical abolitionism in the North, marked by the founding of the anti-slavery journal *Liberator* in 1831. Reflecting mounting concern over slavery, the abolitionist movement constituted the start of a concerted opposition to the institution by a small, but dedicated, number of militant campaigners. Despised in the South, abolitionist leaders, like *Liberator*'s editor, William Lloyd Garrison, were also unpopular in northern states.

Northern whites were convinced of the racial inferiority of African Americans and resented the claims of abolitionists that black slaves had a right to freedom. The grotesque images of blacks perpetrated by minstrel performers confirmed the 'wrong-headedness' of abolitionist arguments. Furthermore, they provided reassurance that blacks would never be able to compete with white workers, either as free labour in the North or as slave labour in the developing western territories.

By the mid-1850s slavery, rather than immigration, was the dominant political concern. Popular culture reflected this change. The publication of the novel *Uncle Tom's Cabin* by Harriet Beecher Stowe constituted 'the media event of the decade'. First appearing in serial form during 1851–2 in an abolitionist journal, *National Era*, the work had enormous impact. In book form it sold 50,000 copies within eight weeks of publication and over 300,000 copies within a year. By the early months of 1853 combined British and American sales exceeded one million.

Uncle Tom's Cabin was groundbreaking in other respects. It was the first recognized American novel to have an African American as its main character. Portraying the horrors of slave life through the story of Uncle Tom, a black slave, the work was a public relations triumph for the abolitionist cause. Northern readers wept on reading of the brutalities of southern plantation life as depicted by Stowe. Sadistic beatings, the enforced break up of families through slave sales and the martyrdom of Tom himself, whipped to death by the evil slaveholder Simon Legree, were enough to melt all but the coldest of hearts.

Given Stowe's intention in writing *Uncle Tom's Cabin*, to expose the evils of slavery, it is ironic that the novel is now most commonly thought of as a source of demeaning stereotypes of African Americans. The central character, Tom, was intended by Stowe to be a quietly heroic figure. Instead, his name has become a term of abuse. It evokes the image of a black man, often elderly, with little or no racial pride, and a deferential loyalty to white authority figures, similar to that bestowed by dogs on their owners.

The novel popularized other stereotypes as well. Stowe's portrayal of the slave child Topsy set a precedent for the enduring image of the 'pickaninny'. This creature possessed a set of identikit characteristics that made it instantly recognizable. Pickaninnies were mischievous and ignorant to the point of being comic. This lack of compre-hension was one of their redeeming features, for it was not that pickaninnies were deliberately naughty, but rather that they were unable to understand the difference between right and wrong at all.

Their physical appearance was bizarre, the typical pickaninny being unwashed, possessing a large grinning mouth, rolling eyes, and an erect hairstyle. In short, this was something scarcely recognizable as human at all. The language used in *Uncle Tom's Cabin* to describe Topsy suggested some kind of composite menagerie. She variously possessed the qualities of an ape, a cat, a dog and a 'glittering serpent'.

In common with many abolitionists Stowe's opposition to slavery did not mean that she was free from the racial prejudices of her age. She believed whites to be mentally and morally superior to blacks and also more physically attractive. Many of the black characters in *Uncle Tom's Cabin* were unappealing to look at. The principal exceptions, George and Eliza, were slaves of mixed-race ancestry whose white bloodline was revealed in their more alluring features. Their dramatic flight from bondage demonstrated that they inherited an Anglo-Saxon longing for liberty that did not exist in the full-blooded African American characters in the novel.

In the South the rise of radical abolitionism in the northern states after 1830 led to the development of a siege mentality. White southerners united against the growing threat. One consequence of this was the development of a systematic proslavery ideology. Once perceived as an embarrassing legacy of British imperial rule, from the 1830s onwards, in journals like *De Bow's Review*, southerners defended slavery as a positive good on economic, political, social, racial and religious grounds.

Central to this thinking was the belief that even black slaves benefited from the 'Peculiar Institution'. This was because in their native African environment blacks lived a bestial existence, prone to cannibalism and other depravities. If slavery denied black Africans their freedom this was a small price to pay in return for the benefits it offered in terms of religious education and instruction in civilized behaviour.

The perception that black slaves possessed no culture or social organization of their own persisted long after the abolition of slavery in 1865. Writing at the end of the First World War the white southern historian Ulrich Bonnell Phillips became recognized as a leading academic authority on the 'Peculiar Institution'. In *American Negro Slavery* (1918), Phillips, himself descended from a slave-owning family, presented an image of an idyllic bygone age. Kindly masters and slaves schooled in Western civilization lived alongside each other in an earthly paradise.

Writing in the 1950s the historian Stanley Elkins presented a grimmer picture. No heaven on earth, slavery, he argued, was more akin to a concentration camp with its inmates engaging in a daily struggle for survival. In some respects, however, Elkins shared Phillip's preconceptions. Black slaves captured in Africa went through a traumatic process of 'shock and detachment' that meant that by the time of their arrival in the United States they had been stripped of all vestiges of their tribal culture. Once settled on a southern plantation they were subject to the 'absolute authority' of the master.

The end product of this experience was not the enlightened bondsman envisaged by Phillips but 'Sambo, the typical plantation slave'. A psychological basket case, Sambo was 'docile but irresponsible, loyal, but lazy, humble but chronically given to lying and stealing'. His 'behaviour was full of infantile silliness', a 'childlike quality that was the very key to his being'.

In the 1960s and the 1970s later historians highlighted the failings of the Elkins thesis. Scholars like John Blassingame, Herbert Gutman, and George Rawick demonstrated that slaves retained elements of West African culture as a defence mechanism that enabled them to preserve their sense of identity in the face of the daily oppression of plantation life. Although the nature, extent and regional variation of West African survivals continue to be a subject of debate the essential validity of these findings is now generally accepted.

Tribal culture lived on in slave music, dance and religion. Children were given African names in addition to those bestowed on them by their white masters. In the South Carolina low country, where there was a large black population, slaves retained elements of West African language in the distinctive 'Gullah' dialect of the region. Women adopted tribal hairstyles and dress, such as the wearing of colourful bandanas or headscarves. These traditions were passed down from generation to generation, ensuring the continuation of African culture even among American-born slaves.

More than simply the preservation of a remote, dead past, survivals of this type were meaningful components of a dynamic slave culture. Folk tales told to slave children about Anansi the Spider and Brer Rabbit contained important lessons in life about how vulnerable insects or animals might prevail over a physically more powerful adversary, like Brer Fox or Brer Bear, by superior wit and clever dissimulation.

The fact that the diaries, journals and letters of southern white planters and overseers contained images of childish slaves consistent with the Sambo stereotype is now recognized by historians as less a reflection of reality than an indication of how effectively slaves learnt such childhood lessons. In conscious acts of role-playing slaves appeared childish and incompetent before white authority figures as a means of avoiding work or escaping punishment.

Planters failed to question such conduct because it reinforced their need to see themselves as benign father figures to the slaves under their control. The alternative, that slaves might be cunning, discontented, possibly to the point of longing for revenge against their oppressors, was so disturbing that it was best not contemplated. Wilful myopia of this sort was to be a recurring phenomenon. Throughout the twentieth century images of African Americans in US popular culture continued to reflect the needs and insecurities of white Americans rather than to represent the realities of black life.

The Reconstruction Era, 1865–77, which followed the end of the Civil War, was a period of adjustment. Southern whites had to come to terms with the abolition of slavery whilst southern blacks had to make the transition from slavery to freedom. US popular culture of the 1870s and 1880s bore witness to these changes and the sense of uncertainty over the future development of the nation.

Groups of travelling actors, or 'Tom Troupes' as they were known, continued to exploit the commercial success of *Uncle Tom's Cabin* by re-enacting scenes from the novel across the United States. The political message of the original work now redundant, these entertainments became contrived and sentimental. Performances concentrated on the death of the angelic white child Eva or the emotional separation of Uncle Tom from wife and family. Tearful wallowing took precedence over characterization, and the simplistic portrayals of Uncle Tom in such tableaux contributed to the emergence of the Tom stereotype.

Minstrel shows continued to be popular, and were performed now not just in the North but also in the South and Mid-west. Troupes became larger in size and productions more lavish. By the 1880s African Americans like James Bland and Billy Kersands began to star in minstrel shows and some all black troupes were formed, such as Callander's Colored Minstrels and the Georgia Minstrels.

If an advance, it was a small one. Black performers were paid significantly less than their white counterparts. Despite their skin colour they were also required to wear burnt-cork make-up. In part this was down to tradition, but it was also because blackface heightened the racial caricatures in minstrelsy. It gave performers an exaggerated appearance of wide, grinning mouths and rolling white eyeballs. The most successful black performers developed routines that emphasized these characteristics. Kersands thus used stunts that demonstrated his ability to insert a cup and saucer, or a set of billiard balls, into his mouth.

More dignified was the success of the Fisk Jubilee Singers. Created as a singing group at the black Fisk College in Nashville, Tennessee, after the Civil War, the Fisk Singers developed a repertoire that included both European classics and plantation melodies. In 1871, under a white instructor, George White, the group embarked on a national tour to raise funds for Fisk, collecting over $150,000. The Fisk singers gave many white audiences in the United States and Europe their first experience of African American spirituals. Inspired by their success other black colleges, such as the Hampton Jubilee Singers, formed in 1872, put together their own vocal ensembles.

The popularity of Jubilee singers, and the continued appeal of minstrelsy, was in part a result of an emerging public nostalgia for the pre-war South in the last quarter of the nineteenth century. This was reflected in the literature of the period. In 1881 the southern white journalist Joel Chandler Harris published a collection of slave Brer Rabbit folklore as *The Songs and Sayings of Uncle Remus*. The anthology ignored the pointed subliminal meaning of the stories. Instead, it was used by Harris to present a romantic image of plantation life. The sentimental appeal was heightened by the format that had the tales being told to a white child by an elderly ex-slave. The images presented by Harris amounted to a kind of 'benign racism' of the sort associated with Harriet Beecher Stowe. Uncle Remus was kindly and likable but also comic, servile and of limited intelligence.

Mark Twain's *The Adventures of Huckleberry Finn* (1885), a work sometimes seen as the quintessential American novel, was also set in the ante-bellum south. A central element of the narrative was the friendship between the young Huck and an escaped slave, 'Nigger Jim'. The Jim character had a number of positive qualities, including love for his family and a longing for freedom.

At the same time the repeated use of the epithet 'nigger' in the novel revealed obvious limitations in the author's thinking on race. Huck was clearly the dominant figure in the relationship. Most of the humorous conversations between Huck and Jim were at the latter's expense and echoed the minstrel show dialogues of the day that Twain admired.

The novel also marked the emergence of a new racial stereotype. The 'Huck Finn fixation', as it has been dubbed by historian Donald Bogle, describes a recurring image in US popular culture of a relationship between a male white character on the fringes of society and a trusty black subordinate. The black servant, for that is what he effectively is, reinforces the self-esteem of his outcast companion and helps him to overcome the emotional anxieties that afflict him.

During the 1880s and 1890s there was a marked deterioration in US race relations. In the South blacks were systematically denied the right to vote and the number of racially motivated lynchings increased in number. Segregation became a part of daily life. Negative popular images of blacks increased in number and intensity.

'Coon songs', which first appeared in the 1880s, surpassed even minstrelsy in their demeaning portrayals of African Americans. The lyrics in these musical entertainments presented blacks as objects of ridicule, and depicted black men in particular as being addicted to the vices of drunkenness, gambling, gluttony and stealing. In a parallel development, 'pseudo spirituals' showed that nothing was sacred, mocking black spirituals and religious beliefs.

The 'coon' craze reached a peak of popularity between 1890 and 1914, becoming almost a national pastime. Accepting the inevitable, a few black artists, like composers James Bland and Ernest Hogan, made commercial gain from the vogue by writing or performing 'coon songs'. The personal cost of this accommodation in terms of racial self-esteem is suggested by the title of Hogan's best-selling composition 'All Coons Look Alike to Me'.

Popular novels of the era were equally unenlightened. In the early years of the twentieth century books in the top ten best-seller list routinely referred to African Americans as 'niggers', 'darkies' or 'jigaboos'. Unsurprisingly, many of these had virulently racist storylines.

The leading writer of this genre was southerner Thomas Dixon Jr. who achieved celebrity status as a result of his race-hate shockers. *The Leopard's Spots* (1902), and *The Clansman* (1905) made him a wealthy man, and they easily outsold *Up From Slavery* (1901), the autobiography of the leading African American spokesperson of the day, Booker T. Washington. In Dixon's books the 'benign racism' of Joel Chandler Harris gave way to a new image of the 'black brute', a violent and malevolent male crazed with sexual desire for white women. In Dixon's lurid imaginings African Americans were not so much an inferior race as a different species, akin to the 'lower order of animals'.

In an unfortunate development, worsening race relations at the end of the nineteenth century coincided with technological advances that made it possible to present negative images of African Americans in ever new, and more damaging, ways. In 1887 Thomas Edison invented the phonograph. In the 1890s a commercial market began to develop for phonograph machines and the cylinder recordings that they played. In keeping with the musical tastes of the day coon songs were among the more popular early recordings.

Occasionally these were even made by black performers, like George W. Johnson's minstrel number 'Whistling Coon' recorded for Edison's own company. More generally, recording companies ignored African Americans altogether. The Columbia Recording Company, founded in 1899, gained commercial success from the sale of records by the Fisk Jubilee Singers but otherwise excluded blacks from its label until after the First World War. The Victor Talking Machine, founded in 1901, was marginally more enlightened, recording a series of comic routines by the black entertainer Bert Williams in 1902–3. In 1914 Victor recorded dance numbers by the black bandleader James Reese Europe and his Society Orchestra but such opportunities were rare for African American performers.

The emergence of the early Hollywood film industry saw the coon stereotype transferred to the screen in the *Rastus* series of short comedies made between 1910–11. Productions such as *How Rastus Got His Turkey*, *Rastus in Zululand* and *Rastus's Riotous Ride*, portrayed the adventures of the incorrigible black character, whose desire to avoid work and responsibility was exceeded only by his appetite for chicken and watermelon.

New technology was accompanied by social transformation. From the 1880s the marketing of manufactured goods in the United States began to change. Country stores stocking only one brand of most products began to be replaced by markets containing a variety of competing labels. Manufacturers responded to this challenge by inventing catchy slogans and using attractive eye-catching packaging.

Racially stereotyped imagery became an especial favourite, evoking romantic pictures of the Old South and reassuring white customers of their racial superiority by depicting deferential black servants. Pictures of African American cooks, butlers and gardeners also imbued products with a sense of authenticity, as blacks were seen as possessing a natural understanding of household work because of their slave heritage.

At the turn of the century the 'Coon Chicken Inns' restaurant chain in Utah, Oregon, and the state of Washington, enticed customers with a logo of a grinning black waiter that appeared both on the exterior of diners and on plates, napkins and menus. In the 1880s the N. K. Fairbanks Company in Chicago created an image of two naked black children, the 'Gold Dust Twins', to promote its Gold Dust washing powder. The implicit promise in the marketing was that the product was so effective that even the black complexions of the twins could be washed 'whiter than white'.

In 1890 'Cream of Wheat' breakfast porridge was adorned with the brand symbol of a smiling black chef. In 1893 Nancy Wilson, an ex-slave, was hired to play the character of 'Aunt Jemima' to promote the sale of pancake mix and breakfast cereal marketed under the same name. By the 1910s the Jemima logo was advertised in every American state and Aunt Jemima products were present on the breakfast tables of over 120 million Americans. A plump, happy, southern plantation cook, the Jemima character became a symbol of black deference and servility

Business cards, common from the 1870s, frequently included degrading representations of blacks. From the 1880s cheap household ornaments produced for a mass market routinely made use of racially offensive language and images. Particularly disturbing was the recurring portrayal of African American children as 'alligator bait' in southern tourist memorabilia. Postcards thus depicted unsuspecting 'pickaninnies' in imminent danger of being eaten alive, whilst novelty tape measures rewound to close with the head of a black child inside the jaws of an alligator.

Supposedly humorous, trashy knick-knacks of this sort embodied a range of damaging stereotypes. They played on the longstanding association of blacks with jungle wildlife in western culture. Equally implicit was the suggested failure of black adults to care for their children, a result of their inability to feel natural parental love and the fact that their offspring were so many in number that it was impossible to keep count of them. 'Pickaninnies' were thus typically featured not alone but in groups of up to eight or more.

Goods manufactured for use by white children helped ensure that racial prejudice was inculcated at an early age. Coon moneyboxes not only encouraged saving but also the belief that all African Americans possessed gaping mouths and wide rolling eyes. In the 1890s the 'Jolly Darkey Target Game', manufactured by the Milton Bradley Company, set players the task of scoring points by throwing balls into the mouth of a black figure. Childhood acquisition of this skill was doubtless an asset for young adults when they encountered fairground variants on the coconut shy that challenged them to 'hit the nigger and win a cigar'.

Representations of blacks in US popular culture were the more damaging at the turn of the century because they coincided with the systematic introduction of racial segregation that reduced the scope for daily interracial contact. Governing bodies in sport followed the lead set by politicians and public opinion. In baseball blacks had competed alongside whites since the early 1870s but, following a boycott by white players in 1887, African Americans were relegated to segregated leagues for the next sixty years. Horse racing was a sport dominated by African Americans between the 1870s and the 1890s. The leading jockey during the 1880s was an African American, Isaac Murphy, and between 1875 and 1904 black jockeys won the prestigious Kentucky Derby thirteen times. In 1904 this track record proved insufficient to ensure their continued participation when the jockey club of New York adopted a policy of refusing to grant licences to black riders. After 1911 participation in the Derby was restricted to whites only.

The modern era of boxing is generally seen as starting in 1882 when John L. Sullivan, 'the Boston Strong Boy', became undisputed world heavyweight boxing champion. Predictably Sullivan refused to accept challenges from any black opponent, as did his successor, 'Gentleman Jim' Corbett, after he defeated Sullivan to take the title in 1892.

Despite such barriers, at the start of the twentieth century boxing survived as one of the few sports where it was possible for blacks to compete against whites. Against the odds on 26 December 1908, in Sydney, Australia, the African American Jack Johnson secured a contest with World Heavyweight Champion Tommy Burns. This reflected the fact that there was a paucity of credible white contenders. The financial terms also heavily favoured Burns, who received $30,000 for the fight compared to a purse of just $5,000 for Johnson. Given that the referee for the contest was his own manager, Sam Fitzpatrick, Burns doubtless felt optimistic about the outcome.

If so he was mistaken. Johnson triumphed with a knockout victory and became the first African American to win the world heavyweight crown. At a time when the dominance of white sportsmen was seen as proof of Anglo-Saxon racial superiority the outcome came as a shock to many white Americans. Surprise gave way to anxiety and despair as Johnson comfortably defended his title against all challengers in the years 1909–12.

Particularly galling was the defeat of former heavyweight champion Jim Jeffries, who had been goaded out of retirement by the press and public opinion to fight Johnson in Reno, Nevada, on 4 July 1910. News of Johnson's victory sparked off outbreaks of racial violence across the nation. Two years later, on 4 July 1912, Johnson despatched his last credible white opponent, 'Fireman' Jim Flynn, in Las Vegas. Concerned at inflammatory newsreel images of yet another Johnson victory, Congress responded by banning the interstate transportation of fight films.

Johnson's brash personality made his successes harder to take for white audiences. He taunted opponents in the ring and delighted in the beatings he inflicted on them. In a personal life that was more public than private the title-holder drank heavily, opened a nightclub in Chicago, the Cabaret de Champion, and drove cars that at the time were considered fast. Worst of all, he openly consorted with a succession of white prostitutes and mistresses and, in 1911, took a white bride, Etta Duryea, who committed suicide on 11 September the following year. For many whites, Johnson was the personification of the black brute depicted by Thomas Dixon Jr.

Responding to the sense of public hysteria created by Johnson's serial seductions, in 1910 Congress passed the Mann Act. The White Slave Traffic Act, as it was also known, forbade the transportation of women across state lines for immoral purposes. Partly inspired by fanciful reports of white women being kidnapped by swarthy foreigners and forced into a life of concubinage, the legislation also targeted Johnson. In October 1912 he was charged with violating the Act because of his affair with a white eighteen-year-old, Lucille Cameron. Even though he went on to marry her, Johnson was convicted in May 1913 and had to flee the country to avoid imprisonment. The same year bills designed to prevent miscegenation, the interracial marriage of blacks and whites, were introduced in ten of the twenty states that still permitted such unions, though none of these were actually passed into law.

In his last major fight, on 5 April 1915, in Havana, Cuba, Johnson was finally vanquished in the ring by another 'great white hope' the 'Pottawatomie Giant' Jess Willard. The outcome has been a source of controversy ever since. Johnson subsequently claimed that he threw the fight for a financial bribe and a covert deal that would enable him to return to the United States without having to go to jail. At the same time, at thirty-seven years old, Johnson was past his prime and, when knocked out by his younger opponent in round twenty-six, he may simply have succumbed to physical exhaustion.

No pardon was forthcoming. Homesick, Johnson returned to the United States in 1920 and served out his jail term. On his release he eked out a living as a fairground boxer and, in an end consistent with his fast lifestyle, died in a car crash in 1946.

In contrast to the larger-than-life Johnson, most African Americans at the end of the nineteenth century lived personal lives hidden from white Americans. Legal separation under 'Jim Crow' segregation laws was reinforced by the continuing rural isolation of many southern communities, in which the majority of African Americans still lived.

Excluded from white bars, theatres and dance halls southern blacks had to create their own entertainment in 'juke joints'. Typically a small wooden building with a corrugated roof, and only the most basic amenities, jukes often constituted the only venue for black social gatherings. In the 1890s the need to provide loud and cheerful music for weekly dance events, with a piano as the only available instrument, led to the emergence of a new style of music, Ragtime. Distinctively African American in origin, rags were vibrant, energetic and often performed to accompany particular dances, like the 'Cakewalk'.

Scott Joplin, the 'King of Ragtime', was born in Texarkana, Texas in 1868 and first earned a living as a professional musician on moving to St Louis, Missouri, in the mid-1880s. Within a few years his piano rags attracted a large following in southern black communities. In 1899 his compositions became available to white audiences when they were published in written form. They became an instant success, his most popular work, 'Maple Leaf Rag', selling more than one million copies in sheet music.

A black artist who had a huge 'crossover' appeal in white society, both in Europe and America, Joplin's career set a precedent for the future. In a recurring phenomenon for African American musicians Joplin's rags provided a source of inspiration for later compositions by white artists, such as Irving Berlin's 'Alexander's Ragtime Band' (1911), who reaped greater commercial reward from them than Joplin himself.

The social and geographic exclusion of blacks from mainstream American life meant that African survivals in black culture continued after the abolition of slavery. This was reflected in the emergence of the 'Blues' in the early years of the twentieth century. Complex in origin, Blues music had its roots in traditional ballads, work 'hollers', sung by black labour gangs during and after slavery, as well as African musical forms and diverse other influences.

Invaluable source material for historians, Blues music provides insights into southern black life of the period. The rustic nature of this existence is indicated by recurring stories and metaphors involving animals. Frequently lyrics empathized with the patient suffering of beasts of burden like mules which, in common with African Americans, were at the bottom of the social order and endured long hours of labour for little reward.

Love and sex were also popular themes, with Blues singers, the majority of whom were male, boasting of their sexual prowess with images of roosters, stallions or writhing black snakes. Women in these lyrics were typically depicted as objects of sexual gratification, heifers, mares and pig-meat, rather than as individuals.

Often Blues singers were lone individuals who travelled across the South working as transient labourers on the railroads, as levee workers building river flood defences, or in the turpentine industry. The solitary nature of this existence is borne out by the highly personalized nature of many Blues lyrics.

Political meaning in the Blues continues to be a source of debate. Often songs appear accommodationist, recounting wrongs and misfortunes which the singer nonetheless accepts with fatalistic resignation. On other occasions the message is more subversive, with the use of coded language to highlight racial injustice. In this vein lyrics referred to white authority figures as 'Mr Charley' or described a segregated neighbourhood as 'bad luck town'. Ultimately, as with many aspects of African American culture, the Blues are perhaps best understood not in terms of accomodationism or resistance, but rather as a survival mechanism that helped blacks to cope with the harsh realities of daily life.

This was to be a recurring phenomenon in the twentieth century. From Jazz in the 1920s and 1930s, through to Disco in the 1970s and Rap in the 1990s, popular music enabled black Americans to bear continuing racial inequalities and social and economic hardship.

Less positively, negative racial stereotypes of African Americans popularized during slavery and the minstrel era were also remarkably enduring. In an epoch of massive social and economic change, and unprecedented technological advances, the portrayals of black Americans in US popular culture continued to be shaped by attitudes dating back at least as far as the 1830s. Paradoxically, the new and highly inventive forms of mass entertainment of the twentieth century – film, radio and television – kept alive the ill-informed and anachronistic traditions of minstrelsy.

CHAPTER ONE

Migration and urbanization, 1915–30

In the early twentieth century the United States was a rapidly changing place. In 1900 the majority of Americans lived in the countryside; by the end of the 1920s over half lived in towns and cities. In 1900 there were just 8,000 cars registered in the United States, and the horse, or horse-drawn vehicles, remained the most common form of private transport. In 1930 over 26.5 million cars were registered and the word horsepower had taken on a different meaning.

The overall impression was one of moving forward. The development of the new discipline of psychiatry provided fresh insights into the human mind. The emergence of professional groups, like social workers and city planners, offered new solutions for the social evils of the day. The period 1900–20 became known as the Age of Progressivism, an era in which it seemed that progress in science, technology and understanding of the human condition might lead to an epoch of contentment and prosperity.

Unfortunately, change was not always for the better. In 1915 the epic *Birth of a Nation* was a landmark in the development of the Hollywood film industry, costing $110,000 to make at a time when the average budget for a film was $20,000. It was over three hours in length at a time when productions usually ran for less than an hour. The film incorporated cinematic techniques that were revolutionary for the day, like tracking shots, close-ups and fade-outs. It ran for ten months in New York City and twenty-two weeks in Los Angeles. More than 25 million people saw the production, and for up to half of these it was the first film they had ever seen. It was also the first film to be screened at the White House, before Woodrow Wilson. A noted historian in his own right, the President endorsed the film as 'writing history with lightning' because of what he regarded as its searing but accurate portrayal of historical events.

The storyline was ambitious, depicting the history of the nation from the days of slavery to Reconstruction as seen through the eyes of two families, the Stonemans from the North and the Camerons from the South. A key message of the film was to highlight the horrors of warfare and the need for the peaceful resolution of political problems. The release of the production in the midst of the First World War gave this message especial poignancy.

Regrettably, other themes in *Birth of a Nation* were less uplifting. The final third of the film, based on Dixon's novel *The Clansman*, portrayed the Reconstruction era after the Civil War as a disaster in the nation's history. It was depicted as a time when self-seeking northern carpetbaggers combined with corrupt southern white scalawags and ignorant ex-slaves to place the South under a form of political despotism in order to plunder the wealth of the region.

The depiction of African Americans was the most offensive aspect of the production. The image of the 'black brute' as popularized by Dixon was brought alive on the screen in the character of Gus, an ex-union army soldier. In one scene Gus sought to force his attentions on the innocent younger daughter of the Cameron family who only escaped rape by committing suicide. The impact of the chase on filmgoers was such that some viewers fired pistols at the screen in an attempt to save the white damsel.

Other black characters, if more sympathetic, were equally demeaning. The faithful retainers who continued to serve the Cameron family after the Civil War reinforced the image of the loyal black slave. The character of the household cook became one of the earliest representations of the jovial, rotund, black mammy, a figure hitherto uncommon, both in the writings of slave-owners and subsequent romanticized portrayals of the ante-bellum south.

Birth of a Nation also marked the first major screen appearance of the 'tragic mulatto', a stereotype that, in literary form, dated back to Harriet Beecher Stowe's *Uncle Tom's Cabin*. Doomed by mixed-race ancestry, the mulatto longed to be accepted into white society, an aspiration that could never be fulfilled because of his or her black bloodline. Embittered and self-loathing, the mulatto served as a warning of the consequences of racial amalgamation.

The release of *Birth of a Nation* occurred at a time when, on average, one African American a week in the southern states was killed, often in horrific fashion, by lynch mobs, most commonly because of ill-founded allegations of sexual assault against white women. The film's glamorous portrayal of the Klan was partly responsible for the rebirth of the 'Invisible Empire' in 1915.

Civil rights leaders and organizations, most notably Booker T. Washington, William Monroe Trotter and the National Association for the Advancement of Colored People (NAACP), came together in a rare show of unity to condemn the film and organize public protests against it. NAACP lawsuits in New York City and Boston sought to have the production banned. The results of these actions were generally unsuccessful. Attempts at prohibition sometimes led to the most inflammatory scenes being cut, but carried the stigma of seeking to restrict freedom of expression. Opponents of the film also suffered the classic dilemma of the advocates of censorship; the more controversial *Birth of a Nation* became, the more people wanted to see it.

The long-term impact of the film was also discouraging. Later filmmakers avoided the portrayal of black characters or racially sensitive issues altogether. The reasoning behind this was more commercial than idealistic. By the 1920s over 50 million Americans went to the cinema every week. Many films were marketed in Europe. Although this offered the prospect of large financial rewards the level of risk also increased, with the average cost of making a film rising to $300,000 by the mid-1920s. Controversial subject matter was therefore generally avoided, lest this lead to failure at the box office.

Film roles requiring the portrayal of black characters were almost non-existent throughout the 1920s. The few parts that were available were almost always as servants, maids or chauffeurs and involved only brief appearances. A slight advance was that by the end of the decade these were usually played by African Americans rather than whites in blackface, as had been the custom in earlier productions, including *Birth of a Nation*. The reason for this change was commercial. Improvements in the quality of film, and a demand from cinemagoers that films look more realistic, meant that the use of burnt-cork make-up was no longer acceptable. An exception to the rule was the release of the first talking picture, *The Jazz Singer* in 1927. Starring Al Jolson in blackface, the film exposed new generations of Americans to the racial caricatures of minstrelsy at a time when it was declining as a form of entertainment.

Another stereotype, the pickaninny, was kept alive in the *Our Gang* comedies of Hal Roach, the first of which was released in 1922. The series focused on the adventures of a group of white and black children but the names of the latter, 'Sunshine Sammy', 'Farina', 'Stymie' and 'Buckwheat', together with their comic appearance, set them apart from their white co-stars.

Small independent African American film companies like the Frederick Douglass Film Company, 1916–20, and the Lincoln Motion Picture Company, 1915–23, tried to provide more dignified portrayals of black characters for African American audiences, but were commercial failures. They were unable to secure the funding needed to meet the high cost of film production. Equally, they found it hard to obtain sufficient outlets for their productions, many theatres up and down the country being solely for whites.

Occasionally, films with blacks in leading roles were made for the white market, but these also failed at the box office, despite the fact that the characters were portrayed in a way designed to meet stereotyped white expectations. *Hearts of Dixie* (1929) thus had an all black cast playing happy slaves on a southern plantation after the Civil War, whilst King Vidor's *Hallelujah* (1928) starred Nina Mae McKinney as a tragic mulatto.

Film was not the only new form of popular entertainment available to Americans. In the 1920s radio emerged as a form of mass communication. Starting with only a few local broadcasters, by 1930 there were more than 1,000 radio stations in the United States with airtime dominated by two major national networks, CBS and NBC.

A strong component of radio broadcasts in the 1920s was the playing of music, either recorded or in live broadcasts from nightclubs, dance halls and hotel ballrooms. Whatever the venue, black musicians were given only a small amount of airtime, particularly on stations affiliated to the national networks. The best opportunities for black performers were on small local stations in large northern cities.

Between 1927 and 1930 Duke Ellington and his Orchestra performed over 200 times on New York stations. Other black musicians, like Fletcher Henderson and Louis Armstrong, also featured. In 1927 Floyd J. Calvin produced the first programme devoted to black journalism on WGBS radio in New York. An hour in length, it was sponsored by an African American newspaper, the *Pittsburgh Courier*.

On WGBC in Chicago *The Negro Hour*, launched by Jack L. Cooper, played recordings by leading black musicians, like Armstrong, Ellington, Henderson and King Oliver. A leading black pioneer in early radio, Cooper went on to become a millionaire and own his own broadcast studio and advertising agency by the end of the 1940s.

Cooper's success was not typical. The Harlem Broadcasting Corporation, the first truly independent African American venture into commercial radio, collapsed within a few years. All major radio stations of the 1920s were white-owned. The unwillingness of white backers to give black artists airtime access ensured that white bands, like the Vincent Lopez Orchestra or Paul Whiteman Band, dominated music shows on early radio.

Often white ensembles played cover versions of numbers created by black bands. These imitations were generally of less intrinsic merit than the originals but were more acceptable to white listeners. This was an important consideration because radio audiences of the 1920s were predominantly white. African Americans comprised less than 15 per cent of the national population. This minority group status was accentuated by economic inequalities. In 1930 only 14.4 per cent of urban black households owned a radio, and in rural districts, where the majority of African Americans still lived, radios were typically owned by less than one per cent of the black population.

The owners of radio stations targeted their broadcasts at white audiences. This was also the case with commercial sponsors of radio shows. In the early 1920s there was little commercial advertising on radio and as late as 1927 advertising funded only 4.3 per cent of US radio stations. By the end of the decade commercial sponsorship became more important. Fear of alienating sponsors, combined with the desire to maximize listening audiences, reinforced the conservatism of station owners in devising broadcasting schedules. In another unfortunate development racist advertising stereotypes were brought to the airwaves. In the late 1920s Quaker Oats used a white actress, Tess Gardella, to play Aunt Jemima, both in a radio marketing campaign and a CBS show devoted to the character.

The use of white actors and comedians to play black characters on radio was essentially a modernized version of blackface minstrelsy, which in its traditional form was in decline by the 1920s. The expansion of radio enabled minstrel stereotypes to live on and opened them up to larger audiences. The most striking example of this was the *Amos 'n' Andy Show*. Devised by two white entertainers, Freeman Gosden and Charles Correll, the production centred on the comic experiences of two black migrants to the north.

The venture had modest beginnings, airing initially on local radio in Chicago as the *Sam 'n' Henry Show*. It was an instant success. In August 1929 the show was given nationwide billing on NBC, with Gosden and Correll receiving a $100,000 contract to perform the show on primetime slots six nights a week. At the height of its appeal 53 per cent of the national radio audience, more than 40 million people, regularly listened to *Amos 'n' Andy*.

One reason for the show's success was its genuinely witty dialogue. It also had contemporary resonance, exploiting the comic possibilities inherent in the transition from rural to urban life, an experience that many Americans shared for real in the 1920s. Less positive, but just as important, the show made use of stereotyped images of African Americans that had been a part of mainstream American popular culture since the advent of minstrelsy. The well-meaning but gullible Amos was a modern version of the 'Jim Crow' character of the 1830s. Similarly, Andy, who was lazy and ignorant, but also domineering and self important, shared many of the traits of 'Zip Coon'.

In sport, memories of Jack Johnson were still fresh. Jess Willard, the new champion, defended his title as little as possible and limited contests to white challengers. Jack Dempsey, who defeated Willard for the title in 1919, also drew the colour line. Gene Tunney, who bested Dempsey in two contests in 1926 and 1927, retired undefeated, leaving the title vacant and the prospect of a black contender seemingly no closer.

In athletics, one of the few other areas of sporting activity in which interracial contests were still possible, black participation at the highest level was virtually non-existent. In 1920 two African Americans made the United States track and field team at the Olympic Games in Antwerp, though neither succeeded in winning a medal. At the 1924 Olympics in Paris three blacks were present in the American track and field team. Dehart Hubbard became the first African American to win a gold medal in an individual event, the long jump, ahead of fellow African American Edward Goudin in second place. If this achievement represented a modest advance it was short-lived. At the 1928 Olympics there were no black competitors in the United States squad.

Largely excluded from sport and the new opportunities created by technological advances in film and radio, African Americans were still affected by the major social and economic changes brought about by industrialization and urbanization in the United States between 1915 and 1930.

Although many large urban centres in the North contained black communities, before the First World War African Americans played a limited part in the population drift to the cities. This changed with the Great Migration of 1915–25 when 1.25 million blacks left the South to seek a new life, in the cities of the North.

There were several reasons for this exodus. The expansion of wartime industries created new job opportunities. At the same time, the war resulted in an end to large-scale immigration from Europe creating labour shortages in northern factories. In contrast, the South experienced economic difficulties. From the 1890s through to the 1920s a new insect pest, the cotton-boll weevil, devastated cotton crops. New generations of black Americans, with no direct experience of slavery, were also less willing than their parents and grandparents to endure the oppressive racial conditions of the South.

The social and cultural impact of the Great Migration was far reaching. Large black ghetto residential districts developed in northern cities, such as Harlem in New York, and the South Side in Chicago. One reason for this was the growth of segregation in the North, making it impossible for black families to move into white neighbourhoods. Finance was also a consideration, with migrants only being able to afford accommodation in the least desirable areas. Often African Americans preferred to live in racially autonomous neighbourhoods that were removed from white surveillance.

Young artists, painters, poets, writers and musicians were drawn to the new ghettos where they were able to meet, exchange ideas and find sources of inspiration. This resulted in a flowering of black cultural achievement that became known as the Harlem

Renaissance. Centred on Harlem, New York, the Renaissance, or New Negro Movement as it was also called, embraced almost all areas of artistic activity but became most closely associated with a talented new generation of black writers and poets. These included Claude McKay, Langston Hughes, Zora Neale Hurston, Jean Toomer and Countee Cullen.

Generally well educated, and from middle-class backgrounds, these artists showed empathy with ordinary black Americans in their writings. They also expressed their anger at racial injustice. Claude McKay's collection of poetry, *Harlem Shadows* (1922), typified this sense of outrage, with poems like 'The Lynching', 'To The White Fiends', and 'If We Must Die'.

Leading Renaissance figures often carried their rebellion against social constraints into their personal lives. Langston Hughes resisted attempts by his parents to persuade him to take up a career in accountancy, giving up his studies at Columbia University to pursue a literary career. Claude McKay became a member of the Communist Party and Countee Cullen rejected the religious values of his father.

The work of Renaissance artists became especially fashionable in white artistic circles in the North. In part this was a conscious act of rebellion as young educated whites from middle-class backgrounds rejected the values of their parents and grandparents. It can also be seen as part of a wider reaction of Americans to the horrors of the First World War.

This took differing forms in various parts of the country. In the South and the Mid-west there was a revival of religious fundamentalism and traditional isolationist values. The country as a whole supported the National Origins Act (1924), placing severe restrictions on immigration to the United States in an attempt to protect the nation from corrupting foreign influences.

The slaughter on the battlefields of Europe demonstrated that advances in technology and human knowledge were not always a force for good. This prompted a romantic interest in primitivism among northern artists and intellectuals. This vogue embodied a romantic longing to escape the complexities of modern life by looking to pre-industrial societies for inspiration.

Black renaissance artists were seen as having a natural affinity for tribal culture because of their African ancestry. Romanticized racial preconceptions of African Americans promoted the belief that they

24

were carefree, spontaneous and possessed natural rhythm. The need to attract funding from affluent white backers sometimes prompted black artists to encourage these perceptions. They could equally be a source of conflict. Langston Hughes fell out with one wealthy patron because of her refusal to accept that he did not feel the 'rhythms of the primitive' running through him, and that although he 'loved the surface of Africa' he 'was not Africa' but 'Chicago and Kansas City and Broadway and Harlem'.

Although writers like Hughes were sustained by white funding the New Negro Movement was more than just a passing vogue. Leading lights in the Movement possessed genuine talent and their work has commanded lasting critical acclaim. Some individuals may have made compromises in their dealings with patrons but this is true of artists throughout history. Frequently, Renaissance artists were not prepared to make concessions, as is reflected in the sharp social observations and eloquent attacks on racial injustice that typify their work.

In a parallel development to the Harlem Renaissance some white writers of the 1920s looked to black life and society for literary inspiration. Dubbed the 'Negrotarians' by Zora Neale Hurston, they included authors and playwrights like Carl Van Vechten, Sherwood Anderson and DuBose Heyward.

In their writings Negrotarians displayed many of the romanticized racial beliefs held by white patrons of the Harlem Renaissance. DuBose Heyward's novel *Porgy* (1925) examined the conflict in a love triangle involving the book's principal characters, Porgy, Bess and her former lover Crown. On the run for murder, Crown was depicted as being animal in instinct, and having a natural affinity with Mother Earth. In 1927 the novel was adapted into a play that ran on Broadway in New York and it was later turned into a musical.

In 1920 Eugene O'Neill's *The Emperor Jones*, portraying the rise and fall of a black dictator in the Caribbean, was another Broadway success, and marked the emergence of a major new talent, Paul Robeson, in the leading role. The play's storyline required that Robeson initially triumph over his white adversaries but the 'natural' racial order was restored with the dictator's ultimate demise, which enabled audiences to savour the 'black brute' receiving his just retribution. In another O'Neill play, *All God's Chillum Got Wings* (1924), Robeson achieved the distinction of being the first black man to play the principal role opposite a white actress in a Broadway production.

Notwithstanding the success of Negrotarian writers most novels in the top ten of the bestseller list during the 1920s avoided racial issues and black characters, although this in itself can be seen as an advance in comparison to the virulent racist imagery that was commonplace in popular novels in the years before the First World War.

One notable development was the publication of *Tarzan of the Apes* (1914), by white Chicagoan Edgar Rice Burroughs. Anticipating the 1920s interest in primitivism, the novel focused on the life of an heir to an English peerage reared as a child by a family of apes in the jungle, following the death of his parents in a plane crash. Despite this start to life the 'natural' aristocracy of race was restored as Tarzan grew up to become master of his domain. Even in black Africa it was a white man who was king of the jungle. In what was to be the first of countless screen adaptations a film version of the book was released in 1918.

Born in 1925, Malcolm X, one of the leading African American icons of the twentieth century, reflected in his 1965 autobiography that as a child he had 'never thought' of 'the black people in Africa'. Instead his 'image of Africa' was as a place of 'naked savages, cannibals, monkeys and tigers and steaming jungles'. Although he claimed to be unable to understand why he had held such perceptions it is not difficult to find a possible explanation.

In the music industry, as with film and radio, there were major developments and technological advances in the period 1915–30. On 30 January 1917, The Original Dixieland Jazz Band, a white ensemble, made the first commercial Jazz record. Released as 'Livery Stable Blues', it went on to sell more than 1 million copies. The Jazz era had begun. It was to dominate American popular music for the next thirty years.

Nick La Rocca, leader of The Original Dixieland Jazz Band, insisted that Jazz was 'strictly white man's music' and owed nothing to 'the Negro race' or anything 'coming from the jungles of Africa'. He should have known better. Coming from diverse roots, Jazz was clearly influenced by marching band music, the music of the black Baptist churches, Ragtime and the Blues. Geographically, it originated in the black quarter of New Orleans where, in the 1890s, an African American musician, Charles 'Buddy' Bolden (1877–1931) became the first acknowledged performer of what can be recognized as Jazz music. Unhappily, Bolden set another precedent, that of the talented Jazz musician destroyed by a life of personal tragedy. Stricken with mental illness in 1907, Bolden spent the rest of his life in an asylum.

Another precursor of Jazz, James Reese Europe, suffered an equally tragic fate. Commissioned as bandleader for the African American 309th 'Hellfire' Infantry during the First World War, Europe's orchestra performed to popular acclaim in France. Seemingly in the early stages of a successful career, in May 1919 Europe was killed in an altercation with another band member.

Following the success of 'Livery Stable Blues' The Original Dixieland Jazz Band became a public sensation. In 1919, the same month that Reese Europe died, the Band embarked on a tour of Britain playing to English audiences and American servicemen stationed in the country. The ensemble continued to perform until 1925 when it disbanded after La Rocca suffered a mental breakdown. By this time more talented performers had overtaken the Band.

On 12 February 1924 a performance of George Gershwin's 'Rhapsody in Blue' in New York City by another all white group, the Paul Whiteman Band, confirmed Whiteman as the 'King of Jazz'. He retained the title throughout the 1920s. Whiteman's success reflected his ability to make Jazz appear respectable. Admired by the young, the initial reaction of older generations to Jazz had been less positive. Professor Henry Van Dyck at Princeton University summed up their mood when he concluded that it was 'not music at all' but merely a 'combination of disagreeable sounds' with 'wilful ugliness' and 'deliberate vulgarity'. In short, parents responded to the new music enjoyed by their children in the way that they would continue to do throughout the twentieth century, with a mixture of horror and incomprehension.

The Whiteman Band helped to allay this anxiety by making Jazz sound more classical in style, closer to European musical forms, but distancing it from its African American roots. Whiteman acknowledged his artistic indebtedness to black performers but, because of segregation, was unable to hire black musicians. Consequently, although the Whiteman Band surpassed all rivals in commercial terms, the most creative, innovative, Jazz music in the 1920s was played by less well-paid black ensembles. The most prominent of these were The Duke Ellington Orchestra and Fletcher Henderson Band, in New York City, and the King Oliver Band in Chicago.

27

Easily the most talented individual performer was the new trumpet sensation, Louis Armstrong, who worked with both Henderson and Oliver. Making his first commercial recording in April 1923, with King Oliver, Armstrong was instrumental in developing the richness and complexity of Jazz in the mid-1920s and in establishing a role for solo performers within bands. In 1926 his release of 'Heebie Jeebies' popularized another innovation, 'scat singing', the mixing and jumbling of words in rhythm with the music.

A different kind of challenge was the need to develop dance styles to accompany the new music. African Americans again provided the inspiration. In 1923 a new black musical revue on Broadway, *Runnin' Wild*, introduced white audiences to the Charleston. In 1928 George 'Shorty' Snowden pioneered the 'Lindyhop' in Harlem. Named in honour of the aviator Charles Lindburgh, the dance also became known as the 'Jitterbug'.

Runnin' Wild was one of a series of black musicals to play on Broadway during the 1920s. During 1921 and 1922 *Shuffle Along* became the hottest show in town, including the songs 'I'm Just Wild About Harry' and 'Love Will Find a Way'. In 1923 *Chocolate Dandies* marked the professional debut of singing and dancing legend Josephine Baker. *Blackbirds*, 1926–8, brought recognition for vocalists Ethel Waters and Adelaide Hall.

Off Broadway, the Cotton Club in Harlem became the nation's most fashionable nightspot. Built in 1918 the club was originally owned by the boxer Jack Johnson. Its fortunes thereafter mirrored the social changes of the day. In the next decade Owney Madden, a notorious gangster, became owner of the club, reflecting the rise of bootlegging and organized crime during the prohibition era of 1919–33.

In some aspects of his business life Madden was more conventional. For most of the 1920s the club hired exclusively black entertainers but, in keeping with the segregated practices of the time, excluded blacks as paying customers. The golden era of the club came in the years 1927–31 when Duke Ellington and his orchestra performed as resident musicians playing numbers like 'Creole Love Call', 'Black and Tan Fantasy', and 'Mood Indigo'.

Born in 1899, Ellington's talents as a composer matched those of Louis Armstrong as a performer. Like Armstrong, he profoundly shaped the development of Jazz during the 1920s and 1930s.

Ellington's professional career, which lasted for more than fifty years, was both prolific and constantly innovative, making him arguably the most influential American composer of the twentieth century.

From modest beginnings at the turn of the century, by the 1920s the record industry had become a massive commercial undertaking. In the mid-1920s more than 100 million phonograph records were sold in the United States every year. Up to 6 million of these were purchased by African Americans, in the form of 'race records' targeted at black customers.

Despite the creation of the first African American owned label, Black Swan, by 'Father of the Blues', W. C. Handy, in 1921, most race records were produced by white-owned companies. These made substantial profits from the African American market. In contrast the black artists who featured on the records received little reward for their labour. Between 1923 and 1933 Blues legend Bessie Smith was paid less than $28,600 by the Columbia label, yet the company made more than $1 million from the sales of her records. Other performers were paid even less, often only a token recording fee.

Although African Americans regularly purchased releases by the leading black Jazz performers most race records sold were by Blues artists. Ironically, a white singer, Sophie Tucker, made the first commercial Blues recording, 'Saint Louis Blues' in 1917. This was the exception to the rule. During the 'Classic Era' of Blues in the 1920s all the major artists were African Americans, including Blues greats like Blind Blake, Blind Lemon Jefferson, Big Bill Broonzy, Gertrude 'Ma' Rainey, as well as Bessie Smith. In their music these performers remained close to their cultural roots. Blues lyrics also focused on subjects that were familiar to African Americans in their daily lives.

The Great Migration of 1915–25 not only helped to further the geographical spread of the Blues, but also provided fresh sources of inspiration. Often lyrics focused on the longing of singers to escape the South by journeying 'Chicago Bound' to the North. Trains, a symbol of freedom for African Americans from the days of the abolitionist 'Underground Railroad' before the Civil War, evoked bittersweet feelings. A means of escape, the railways were also a source of pain, dividing migrant passengers from loved ones left behind.

Urban life in the North provided new imagery to explore familiar themes. In songs recounting their sexual prowess Bluesmen began to describe themselves as 'chauffeurs' rather than 'roosters', and boasted not of black snakes but the size of the range in their kitchen.

Black tenants in northern apartments who lacked sufficient money to pay the landlord at the end of the week often made up the shortfall by holding 'House Rent' or 'Social Whist' parties. Friends and neighbours paid a small entrance fee to attend the gathering in return for cheap alcohol, food, and entertainment by a Blues singer. This both ensured the further spread of the music within the North and provided material for future compositions about the 'House Rent Blues'. African American culture in the 1920s, as it had been during slavery, was not only rich and diverse but also a meaningful part of daily life.

CHAPTER TWO

The Great Depression and the Second World War, 1930–45

In late October 1929 share prices on Wall Street in New York City fell dramatically. Hopes that this might be no more than a temporary setback were soon extinguished as they continued to plummet through November and December and into the New Year. The Wall Street Crash, as it became known, deepened into the Great Depression. The decade-long party that had been the 1920s was over. For many, like the urban ghetto poor, African American sharecroppers, and small farmers of both races in the South and the Mid-west, it had never begun. Even during the good times of the 1920s they lived in poverty.

In the early 1930s other Americans shared the same experience. The national unemployment rate rose from 1.5 million in 1929 to 13 million by 1933. Almost every household in the country was affected in some way.

The entertainment industry did not escape. Baseball colossus George 'Babe' Ruth was forced to accept a pay cut with the New York Yankees. In New York City alone over 100 dance halls closed, as did half the theatres on Broadway. Record sales fell from 100 million a year to just 6 million. Okeh, Gennett and Paramount records all went bust, and the RCA Victor Talking Machine Company ceased producing record players.

Jazz, associated with the excesses of the 1920s, was an unhappy reminder of days gone by, and suffered accordingly. In March 1933, the final lifting of Prohibition, by incoming President Franklin Roosevelt, at least enabled Americans to lawfully seek consolation for their troubles in alcohol. It also meant that illicit 'speakeasies' of the 1920s, that had provided venues for Jazz musicians, were surplus to requirements. The first introduction of jukeboxes, in

1933, did not help the cause of live musicians either, though their provision of cheap entertainment befitted the austere nature of the time. Even the most celebrated performers were compelled to face the financial realities of the day. Paul Whiteman laid off ten members of his thirty-man band and imposed a 15 per cent pay cut on the rest.

Black musicians and artists suffered badly. The Harlem Renaissance came to an abrupt end as white patronage was cut off. Performers who relied on the African American market for most of their income were hit hardest of all. Traditionally the 'last hired' during times of economic growth, and the 'first fired' in times of recession, most black Americans lacked sufficient income for the necessities of life, let alone expenditure on leisure.

In the 1920s the average yearly sales for a race record was 10,000 copies. This fell to 2,000 copies in 1930, and just 400 copies in 1932. The classic age of Blues was over. Even performers like Bessie Smith and Ma Rainey struggled to make a living. A positive development was that the Great Depression provided new inspiration for Blues lyrics and gave deeper meaning to existing compositions, like Bessie Smith's poignant 'Nobody Knows You When You're Down and Out'. This was scant consolation. For some the hard times proved too much. In 1938 King Oliver died, as did Ma Rainey the following year, whilst Bessie Smith herself was killed in a car accident in 1937.

Others fared better, but at a personal cost. Throughout the Great Depression, as he had done since 1925, Duke Ellington relied on a white manager, Irving Mills, to obtain bookings and record deals. In a familiar variant on the theme of 'black roots, white fruits' Mills received 45 per cent of the profits, both from Ellington's compositions and performances by Ellington's orchestra. It was not until 1939, when economic recovery was underway, that the Duke felt confident enough to dispense with the services of Mills.

Louis Armstrong also relied on a white manager, Joe Glaser, to see through the 1930s. 'Satchel Mouth' or 'Satchmo', as Armstrong was known, summed up the realities of the time for black entertainers with the saying 'always keep a white man behind you', who will put his hand on your shoulder and say 'that's my nigger'. In public, as well as behind the scenes, Armstrong was forced to make compromises. In a succession of stage and film appearances he adopted a clownish persona with exaggerated grins and popping eyeballs. Uncomfortably reminiscent of minstrel stereotypes from the preceding century, a low-point in these per-formances came in his screen serenade of a horse with the song 'Jeepers Creepers'.

Duke Ellington and his orchestra made a number of cameo appearances in Hollywood films during the 1930s, but the Duke always maintained his elegant, dignified demeanour. Unfortunately, the parts played by Armstrong were more typical of the screen roles open to African Americans. Most commonly, blacks, when they appeared at all, were cast as servants or comic buffoons.

Broadway dancer Bill 'Mr Bojangles' Robinson played a butler opposite the young Shirley Temple in *The Littlest Rebel* (1935). Willie Best and Mantan Moreland both made a career out of playing comic coon characters, following the example set by the most well known practitioner of the genre, Stepin Fetchit. After making his debut in *Hearts in Dixie* (1929), Fetchit went on to become the archetypal coon in some twenty-six films between 1929 and 1935, developing a trademark character with a slouching posture, shuffling gait, and a look of innate stupidity.

Serious acting roles for blacks were rare, and when they did arise were stereotyped. In *Imitation of Life* (1934), Louise Beavers played the part of a loyal and plump family cook, Aunt Delilah, in a feel-good movie that typified Hollywood's response to the Depression. Displaying culinary skills of which Aunt Jemima might have been proud, she overcame economic adversity by marketing her unique pancake recipe. Refusing to accept any reward for herself, Delilah gave all the profits earned from this success to her white employer. Delilah's daughter, Peola, played by Fredi Washington, did not share her mother's servile contentment. The source of the light skinned Peola's unhappiness was not the squandering of a small fortune, but her desire, as a tragic mulatto, to be accepted as white.

A box office hit, *Imitation of Life* helped to inspire the release of *The Green Pastures* (1936) with an all-black cast. Another com-mercial success, the film was sentimental and racially stereotyped. In a bizarre fantasy, scenes from the Bible and life in heaven were re-enacted in the plantation South, the setting least likely to be regarded as an earthly paradise by most African Americans.

In another exotic location Olympic swimming champion, Johnny Weissmuller, made his first appearance as the 'King of the Jungle' in *Tarzan of the Apes* (1932). The creator of Tarzan's famous jungle call, Weissmuller became the actor most remembered for playing the role. In his search for a soul-mate he managed to find a white partner, even in black Africa, though the role of Jane, played by Maureen Sullivan, seemed to be less that of a wife than an admiring audience for Weissmuller's narcissistic pouch posing.

The roles of blacks in the Tarzan films were even more restricted, being confined to savages or porters. Apart from relieving their white masters of physical burden their main purpose was apparently to be eaten alive or horribly put to death before the intervention of Weissmuller, just in time to ensure that no white member of the party suffered such a fate.

In *King Kong* (1933) the message was similar. Black tribal characters on the mysterious tropical island, that was the setting for much of the film, were bestial and uncivilized. These qualities were reflected in the fact that they worshipped a giant ape, Kong, as a god and made human sacrifices to it.

Significantly both Kong and the tribal chief became besotted with the blond beauty of actress Fay Wray. Although subjected to physical danger as a result, it was inevitable that she would finally find happiness in the arms of a blue-eyed, Nordic looking, sea captain. Tall, erect, and with a square jaw that jutted out so far that it almost suggested physical deformity, the hero would not have been out of place as the Aryan lead in a Nazi propaganda film.

More realistic attempts to portray black life and characters were largely confined to the work of the independent black filmmaker Oscar Micheaux. Constantly struggling against financial adversity and a lack of box office outlets, he made a series of low-budget productions for African American audiences, even at the height of the Depression. In a career that lasted from 1919 to 1948 Micheaux defied all odds, releasing some thirty-four films. Denied the recognition that he deserved during his lifetime, he provided a rare alternative perspective to mainstream Hollywood productions and became a source of inspiration for later generations of black filmmakers.

Opportunities for blacks on radio in the 1930s remained limited, and in some respects worsened. This was the result of a variety of factors. The Depression forced many small independent stations to close down. By the mid-1930s the two national networks, NBC and CBS, directly or indirectly controlled 97 per cent of prime-time broadcasting. More conservative than smaller broadcasters, they were less likely to allow blacks airtime. Moreover, when black performers did appear on national radio the networks often received protests from southern affiliates.

Sponsors also exercised more influence in the 1930s. In 1934 NBC and CBS earned more than $75 million in advertising revenue, and all prime-time shows had one or more backers. These sponsors were unwilling to fund programmes with African Americans in a leading role lest their product be perceived as 'black oriented' and shunned by white customers.

The pressure to exclude blacks was reinforced by organized labour. The American Federation of Musicians (AFM), the Radio Writers Guild (RWG) and the American Federation of Radio Actors (AFRA) all excluded blacks from membership. Shows with African Americans thus risked the threats of regional protests from the South, a loss of advertising revenue and labour troubles. Added to this was the danger that these productions might be unpopular with white audiences.

Under the circumstances it was safer for radio executives to exclude blacks altogether. This conclusion was borne out in the experience of the few programmes that were made with African Americans as hosts or in a leading role. In 1933 *The Ethel Waters Show* was cancelled by NBC after a few weeks following a boycott threat from the network's southern affiliates. Another NBC pilot, *Quizzicale* with Cab Calloway, was dropped because of the failure to attract a sponsor. In 1937 *The Louis Armstrong Show* on CBS was pulled after thirteen weeks because of poor ratings.

Albeit depressing, this was a predictable fate as Satchmo was pitted against *The Jack Benny Show*, a popular and established programme that aired on CBS at the same time. Ironically, Eddie Anderson, as Benny's butler, Rochester, became one of the few African Americans to feature regularly on national radio in the 1930s. Benny and Anderson went on to reprise their roles in a series of Hollywood films.

Resourceful and quick witted, Rochester sometimes outsmarted his employer, making the part a breakthrough in the way that blacks were depicted on radio. At the same time Anderson's role was still that of a servant. An assistant to the unconventional Benny in his various escapades and adventures, the relationship between the two men was a variant on the Huck Finn complex.

Although blacks themselves were denied airtime, comic portrayals of African American life by white performers, as in the

1920s, remained popular. The *Amos 'n' Andy Show* continued to run throughout the 1930s and the Second World War. Regularly at or near the top of audience rating lists, the show became the longest running series in the history of US radio broadcasting.

The response of African Americans to *Amos 'n' Andy* was mixed. In 1931 black journalist Robert Vann at the *Pittsburgh Courier* launched a national campaign against the show and collected a petition with some 740,000 signatures demanding that it be pulled. The programme's high listening figures ensured that this demand was unsuccessful. Moreover, some black opinion-formers rallied to the show's defence, like Robert Abbott of the black newspaper the *Chicago Defender*. Sensitive to charges of racism, the white leads in the series, Gosden and Correll, regularly appeared in photo opportunities with black children and celebrities. They sponsored black charity events in the Southside in Chicago, and Harlem in New York City, and were personal friends of Abbott.

Another factor that helped defuse criticism was that *Amos 'n' Andy* was only one of a number of comedy shows that lampooned African Americans. The success enjoyed by Gosden and Correll encouraged a spate of imitators who went on to achieve celebrity status in their own right, like *Pick 'n' Pat* which played first on NBC and later on CBS. In 1939 *Pick 'n' Pat* even topped Gosden and Correll in the national ratings. In 1935, when Tess Gardella gave up the part of Aunt Jemima, Quaker hired another white actress, Harriet Widmer, to take over the role. At the end of the decade the male white entertainer Marlin Hurt launched a new comic black character, the rotund housekeeper Beulah.

Opportunities for real-life African Americans on radio were scarce both at national and local level. A notable exception was the continued success of African American broadcaster Jack Cooper in Chicago. The 'father of black radio', in 1931 Cooper pioneered the early development of the disc jockey format on WSBC in the city. In 1932 he launched the first successful black-run radio company Jack L. Cooper Presentations, which was followed by the creation of the Jack L. Cooper Advertising Company in 1937.

On national radio coverage of sporting events was one of the few occasions when black Americans might be given primetime airing. Excluded from most forms of competition by segregation, in a minority of sports, most notably athletics and boxing, blacks were still able to test their abilities against whites.

The staging of the 1932 Olympics in Los Angeles provided increased opportunity for participation by African American athletes. Black Americans won a total of five medals, more than in any previous Olympiad, with Eddie Tolan taking gold in the 100 metres and the 200 metres, Ralph Metcalfe silver in the 100 metres and bronze in the 200 metres, and Edward Gordon gold in the long jump.

The 1936 Games in Berlin remain one of the most memorable Olympiads of the modern era. In a significant development nineteen African Americans made the US track and field team, more than three times the number that had competed at Los Angeles. Even more striking, the best-known member of the US squad, and the athlete most remembered in connection with the Games, was also African American, the track and field star Jesse Owens.

Less positively, the 1936 Olympics provided a showcase for the Nazi regime of Adolf Hitler to impress world opinion with the German organization of the Games and provide proof of the Führer's belief in the superiority of Aryan athletes. In popular mythology the Games are remembered as an individual conflict of wills between Owens and Hitler.

In the arena Owens was triumphant, winning four gold medals, in the 100 and 200 metres, the long jump, and the 4 × 100 metre relay, each victory setting a new Olympic record. A remarkable achievement in its own right, this success has been accorded even greater status in sporting legend. Owens has been credited with demonstrating the falseness of Hitler's racial theories, and proving the superiority of the American way of life over Nazi totalitarianism. By this interpretation Hitler was so enraged by this propaganda setback that he snubbed Owens, by refusing to shake hands with him, and stormed out of the Olympic arena.

Although appealing, this scenario is inaccurate. On the opening day of the Games, on 2 August, Hitler had publicly congratulated several gold medal-winning athletes, including two Germans and a Finn, inviting them to his private box in the stadium. Henri de Baillet-Latour, President of the International Olympic Committee (IOC), expressed concern, advising Hitler that, as head of state of the host nation, it was his duty to remain impartial. This left the dictator with the choice of congratulating all gold medal winners or none. He opted for the latter course. When Owens won the first of his gold medals on the second day of the Games Hitler, even if willing, was not in a position to publicly congratulate him as protocol prevented him from doing so.

Given Hitler's views on race there can be little doubt that he was displeased at Owens' success. Following the advice given him by Baillet-Latour he did continue to meet some athletes, mostly Germans, in private. This included Lutz Long, the German silver medallist in the long jump, but not Owens, who had bested Long for the gold medal. This was despite the fact that public opinion, even in Germany, regarded Owens as the outstanding performer of the Games.

At the same time, in 1936 Hitler was seeking to project an image of himself as a respectable statesman. Needing no lessons in the importance of public relations, it is unlikely that he would have been willing to let his personal feelings jeopardize this objective. This view is borne out by Nazi initiatives relating to the Olympiad. During the course of the Games the authorities in Berlin were careful to conceal evidence of anti-Semitism in the city. In the aftermath of the Olympiad Josef Goebbels, Nazi Minister of Propaganda, instructed the German press to give Owens favourable publicity to neutralize foreign criticism of the Nazi regime as bigoted and unsporting. Leni Riefenstahl, Hitler's favourite filmmaker, made Owens a focus of attention in her cinematic record of the Games, *Olympia* (1936).

After the Second World War Jesse Owens supported the legend of the Hitler snub, because that was what journalists and the American public preferred to believe. In 1936 he had discounted such reports, even suggesting that Hitler, from the vantage of his private box in the stadium, had smiled and waved at him.

If Hitler's conduct during the Games was different from that remembered in popular mythology, the Olympiad was also less than a vindication of American values. In the medal tables for the Games, the first in which a record was kept of the tally for each competitor nation, there was no doubt as to the overall victor. Germany with a haul of thirty-three gold medals, twenty-eight silver and thirty bronze easily surpassed all other countries. The United States, with twenty-four gold medals, twenty silver and twelve bronze, was in second place.

Moreover, even the splendid individual achievement of Owens was touched by controversy. The final gold medal for the 'ebony antelope', as he was dubbed in the American press, came in the 4 × 100 metre relay, an event in which he had not been scheduled to run. On the eve of the final Owens, together with fellow black athlete Ralph Metcalfe, were substituted for Sam Stoller and Martin Glickman in the US relay team. In respect to Owens, his outstanding run of form made such a change understandable, but the case for introducing Metcalfe was less compelling. The fact that Stoller and Glickman were the only two Jewish athletes on the US track and field team created suspicions of anti-Semitism, or moral cowardice in kow-towing to the prejudices of the Nazi hosts.

Another unpleasant aspect to Owens's victories was that, if not snubbed by Hitler, he did experience racial slights in the United States, both before his departure for the Games and after his return. In common with other African Americans he endured the racial discrimination and segregation that was a daily part of American life.

Unlike white Olympic celebrity Weissmuller, Owens was unable to cash in on his success. In the absence of more lucrative offers in advertising and entertainment he was obliged to accept a retainer to support the Republican Party in the 1936 elections and to take part in demeaning publicity stunts, such as racing against a horse.

In boxing the retirement of Gene Tunney in 1928 marked a low point in the sport. Tunney was followed by a succession of lacklustre holders of the title. At least one, Primo Carnera, was tainted by links with organized crime. This situation, combined with the receding memory of Jack Johnson, created openings for black contenders. The opportunity was seized by Joe Louis, the son of an Alabama sharecropper, who went on to hold the world heavyweight title in an unbroken twelve-year period between 1937 and 1949.

One of the most highly regarded champions in boxing history, Louis was the only African American sportsman in the 1930s to surpass the celebrity status achieved by Jesse Owens. Like Owens, he became a symbol of American national pride in two sporting contests with a champion from Nazi Germany, Max Schmeling.

The first of these took place in New York City on 18 July 1936. The contest was an eliminator to select a challenger for the reigning World Champion James Braddock. Victorious in all fights since the start of his professional career in July 1934, Louis was odds on favourite. The American press regarded Schmeling, a former World Champion, as past his best.

Defying the odds, Schmeling defeated Louis in a twelfth-round knockout. On his return to Germany he was feted as a national hero by the Nazi regime and hailed as proof of Aryan sporting supremacy. Hitler, who had praised the character building qualities of boxing in his autobiography *Mein Kampf*, honoured Schmeling with a personal audience.

Schmeling's victory was supposed to give him the right to fight for the world title against Braddock, a contest the German was likely to win. At this point boxing politics and national pride intervened to alter the course of events. Ignoring his obligation to fight Schmeling, Braddock instead chose to defend his title against Louis, on 22 June 1937, for a considerably larger purse. Predictably, Louis won the contest and was hailed as the new champion. Back in Europe the wronged Schmeling protested. The German camp asserted that by breaking his contractual commitments Braddock had ceded the world title to Schmeling by default. Legally and morally there was good justification for this claim, but in the American dominated boxing establishment, and among US public opinion, Schmeling's case went unheeded.

It was clear that only a second Louis–Schmeling fight would be sufficient to resolve the issue. Louis himself admitted that he did not feel that he would be the true champion until he had vanquished the German in the ring. The rematch, on 22 June 1938 in New York City, removed any doubt. In a crushing victory Louis despatched Schmeling in the first round. Despite the brevity of the contest the beating meted out by Louis was so severe that Schmeling required a period of hospitalization after the fight and had to be carried on a stretcher to catch his flight home. In Germany radio stations terminated coverage of the fight once the outcome of the contest became clear. On his return to the Fatherland the Nazi establishment shunned Schmeling as a disgraced fallen hero.

In the United States Louis's victory was seen as a triumph of American virtue over the evil ideology of Nazi Germany. This perception is both understandable and over-simple. In the case of Schmeling it is also unfair. Although used by Hitler and Goebbels for propaganda purposes he was no Nazi thug. Schmeling always sought to downplay the political dimension to his fights with Louis. He also retained the services of a Jewish manager, Jim 'Yussel the Muscle' Jacobs, despite obvious pressure to replace him. Further evidence of Schmeling's principled conduct came during the Second World War when he aided Jewish refugees to escape the Holocaust. In short, Schmeling was a decent individual who had the misfortune to live under an odious political regime.

In the United States African Americans everywhere shared Louis's despair in his 1936 defeat and rejoiced in his victory two years later. The initial response of white Americans was more mixed. Many white sports journalists proclaimed Schmeling a hero in 1936 and the German received hundreds of telegrams of congratulation from American admirers, especially in the South. Sports pundits dismissed Louis as a spent force, and former World Champion Jack Dempsey declared that he would never defeat a good fighter again.

Two years later these sentiments were forgotten, but they attest to the fragile nature of Louis's relationship with white public opinion in the United States. Both in and out the ring Louis constantly had to regulate his conduct to avoid giving offence. When defeating white opponents he avoided displaying any sign of pleasure. Impassive in the ring, he was generous to vanquished opponents in post-fight interviews and modest in assessing his own achievements.

Always, Jack Johnson was the negative role model that Louis and his handlers consciously sought to avoid. Louis did not drink to excess; he avoided driving at speed in fast cars, and did not have periodic run-ins with the authorities. Above all he did not have sexual relationships with white woman. Ironically, Louis shared Johnson's weakness for extramarital affairs, but confined his attentions to African American women. Consequently, these liaisons went unreported in the white press.

Ultimately won over by Louis's deferential manner, white sports reporters still revealed their prejudices even as they bestowed praise upon him. Accounts of his fights constantly reminded audiences of his racial ancestry. He was the 'mahogany mauler', a 'sepia slugger', or the 'brown bomber'. As with the 'ebony antelope', Jesse Owens, reports linked him to the untamed African wilderness. He was a predatory animal, or a 'jungle killer', despite the fact that Louis clearly had no experience of any such environment in his Alabama childhood.

By 1935–6 Americans had survived the worst of the Great Depression. Large-scale unemployment persisted until the early 1940s but economic conditions were improving. In the 1936 Presidential election incumbent Franklin Roosevelt achieved a landslide victory over Republican challenger Alf Landon.

In popular music the new optimism was reflected in the emergence of Swing. A new style of Jazz performance, Swing defied easy definition but was characterized by a lively tempo and an easy rhythm that made it a natural accompaniment for dancing. In some ways it also moved Jazz away from its African American roots.

Commercially, the most successful exponents of the new genre were white musicians like Glenn Miller and the media dubbed 'King of Swing', Benny Goodman. At the same time black performers also benefited from the revival in popular music, most notably Duke Ellington, Cab Calloway, Chick Webb and the Count Basie Band. The new vocal talents of Ella Fitzgerald, with Webb and Billie Holliday, recruited by Basie, added to the appeal of their respective ensembles.

Generally, black bands were still restricted to inferior venues and received lower financial rewards than their white counterparts. A notable advance, however, was that by the late 1930s some white bandleaders began to incorporate black performers into their ensembles. In 1937 The Benny Goodman Quartet included two black musicians Teddy Wilson and Lionel Hampton. The massive popularity enjoyed by Goodman demonstrated that white audiences, even in the South, were prepared to accept integrated ensembles. Other white bandleaders, like Gene Krupa and Artie Shaw, followed Goodman's example and hired black artists. The downside to this development was that black bands faced the risk of losing their best performers to better paid white ensembles, as reflected in Benny Goodman's recruitment of Duke Ellington's trumpet star, Cootie Williams, in 1940.

By 1939 record sales in the United States had recovered to an annual total of 50 million. In another notable development the same year Billie Holiday released 'Strange Fruit', a poignant condemnation of lynching and the song that was to become her personal trademark. The success of the record, which reached sixteenth spot in the national charts, was another sign of a slight improvement in US race relations. Significantly, the numbers of lynchings in the United States, which had been falling since the start of the century, markedly declined during the 1930s. By the end of the decade reports of the crime were rare.

A less welcome development was the renewed output of black memorabilia, trashy ornaments and knick-knacks that portrayed demeaning stereotypes of African Americans. Aptly described as 'contemptible collectibles' by historian Patricia Turner, these had largely ceased production in the early 1930s. By the end of the decade hope of renewed prosperity revived the market for such merchandise. However, the new products were generally slightly, but noticeably, less extreme in character. Although still racially offensive, the mouths on figurines were not quite as gaping. Eyes did not pop so blatantly, and mammies were a little less obese.

In the cinema growing optimism about the future was reflected in the release of the self-proclaimed 'greatest film of all time', *Gone With The Wind* (1939), based on the 1936 Pulitzer prize-winning book of the same name by Margaret Mitchell. Ironically, Mitchell's novel was one of the few books on the national bestseller list in the period 1930–45 that contained a significant reference to African American characters. The other notable exception was Lillian Smith's *Strange Fruit* (1944), a novel focusing on the murder of an innocent black youth by a white lynch mob in the South.

The cinematic version of *Gone With The Wind* took two years to make at a cost of over $4 million. Operating on a lavish scale, the production used some 2,400 extras, 1,100 horses and 375 other livestock. Fortunately for Director David O. Selznick the film was a massive success, both with critics and the general public. It won ten Oscars, including an award to Hattie McDaniel for best supporting actress, the first Oscar to be awarded to an African American. At the box office some 25 million Americans saw the film during 1939–40.

The film storyline centred on the experiences of a southern white family during the Civil War. In comparison to *Birth of a Nation* it provided modest grounds for encouragement in its handling of racial issues. There were no malicious black brutes. References to the Ku Klux Klan were pointedly omitted, even though the Klan had been portrayed in a favourable light in the original novel. For these reasons there were no major protests by the NAACP or other civil rights organizations on the film's release.

If the film showed the distance that Hollywood had travelled it also revealed the depressing length of the journey still to go. All the black characters in the production were comic stereotypes. Intellectually inferior to the whites they served, they were content to be slaves. Emancipation at the end of the Civil War came as an unwelcome disruption to their existence.

Such distorted images of the nation's past were the more damaging because, for once, the Hollywood interpretation of history was upheld by professional historians of the day. The white southern historian, Ulrich Bonnell Philips, was regarded as a leading authority on the ante-bellum South during the 1920s and 1930s. In his most important works, *American Negro Slavery* (1918) and *Life and Labor in the Old South* (1929), he portrayed slave plantations before the Civil War as earthly paradises peopled by kind masters and happy, well cared for slaves.

Historians of the Reconstruction era, like Francis Butler Simkins and Robert H. Woody, confirmed this one-sided point of view. They portrayed the period after the Civil War as a time of national shame. According to this interpretation ignorant, but politically enfranchised, freed slaves were manipulated by corrupt white southerners, the 'Scalawags', and avaricious Yankee 'Carpet-baggers'. Subjecting the defeated South to political tyranny, these groups plundered the region of its remaining wealth and persecuted native whites.

Respected in the nation's universities, the views of Phillips, Simkins, Woody and others were hailed as an accurate account of the nation's past. Their views were replicated in standard history textbooks and school primers. Teachers, academics, popular novelists, like Mitchell, and filmmakers combined to deny Americans a true understanding of their heritage.

African Americans in particular were denied any pride in their ancestry. Malcolm X, who was a high-school student in the 1930s, recalled how, when he was a student in the seventh grade, black history had been covered in one paragraph. He concluded that it would be impossible to find an American adult of his generation who knew 'anything like the truth' about the role of black Americans from reading the standard history books.

The entry of the United States into the Second World War, in December 1941, had a mixed impact on African Americans and popular culture. In film the administration of Franklin Roosevelt established a Bureau of Motion Pictures within the Office of War Information to ensure that cinematic images supported the war effort. Filmmakers rallied to the cause. Almost one third of all Hollywood productions between 1942–4 provided an uplifting portrayal of some aspect of the war.

In this spirit of unity Hollywood executives met with NAACP delegates in 1942 and pledged to abandon racial stereotypes. In practical terms this resulted in an increased number of small, but sympathetic, roles for African Americans in Hollywood productions. These included Kenneth Spencer as a GI in *Bataan* (1943), Rex Ingrams in the desert adventure *Sahara* (1943), and Canada Lee as one of the survivors of a torpedoed ship in *Lifeboat* (1944). More memorably, Dooley Wilson, in a variant of the Huck Finn complex, featured as the piano player confidante of Humphrey Bogart in *Casablanca* (1943).

The casting of Dooley highlighted the fact that, other than small patriotic roles, the parts most open to blacks in film during the war years were brief appearances as musical entertainers. This created opportunities for morale boosting cameo performances by black celebrities like Louis Armstrong, Duke Ellington and the new singing star Lena Horne.

Less high-minded was the calculation that one or two musical numbers in a nightclub setting, decontextualized from the plot, could be effortlessly cut from a film when it played before southern white audiences. Albeit cynical, such thinking was prompted by box office reality. The South made up a sizeable part of total cinema audiences. Good viewing figures in the region could be crucial to the success or failure of a film. Ominously, the two major productions during the war years with an all black cast, *Cabin in the Sky* (1943), and *Stormy Weather* (1943), were both box office disappointments.

Small film parts were a welcome source of income for musicians as their industry suffered new hardships during the war. Black-outs and late night curfews shut dance halls and nightclubs early. A 20 per cent entertainment tax closed ballrooms across the nation. Road tours, which had been a lifeline for many black performers in the 1930s, were precluded by wartime rationing of rubber and gasoline. Musicians were drafted, leaving bands short of key members.

A less obvious woe was a wartime shortage of shellac. A product secreted by a tree crawling insect in India, shellac was a vital ingredient in the making of 78 rpm records. At the height of the shortage consumers had to return an old record when buying a new one so that it could be recycled. Record companies targeted their reduced output at the most popular markets. This resulted in cutbacks in specialized fields like race records.

Trade union conflicts were another problem. In 1940 the American Society of Composers and Publishers (ASCAP), which protected the royalty rights of its members when their work was performed in public, entered into a dispute with the National Association of Broadcasters (NAB). Refusing to pay increased fees, the NAB, representing some 600-radio stations, formed its own per-forming rights organization, Broadcast Music Incorporated (BMI), and boycotted the playing of work by ASCAP members.

In 1942 a different dispute broke out between recording com-panies and the American Federation of Musicians (AFM). In an attempt to secure larger royalties the AFM ordered its members to stop making records, with the exception of 'V-discs' intended for servicemen. The ban was not lifted until November 1944. Vocalists were the major beneficiaries. Singers did not join in the embargo being members of a different union, the American Federation of Television and Radio Artists (AFTRA). Recording companies turned to issuing releases by singing artists with backing groups. Soloists like Bing Crosby, Perry Como, Doris Day and Frank Sinatra attracted a major public following.

Like Hollywood, the radio networks encouraged feelings of unity. In 1942 and 1943 respectively sympathetic black characters were introduce into leading soaps, *Our Girl Sunday* and *The Romance of Helen Trent*. *Men O'War*, a patriotic weekly musical review made by the navy with a cast of black sailors, aired on CBS. In another CBS broadcast, made in the wake of the 1943 Detroit race riot, Republican Wendell Wilkie delivered *An Open Letter on Race Hatred*. The former presidential candidate compared the white vigilantes who had attached blacks in the city to Nazi thugs.

An unlikely catalyst for racial conflict in Detroit and other northern cities in 1943 was the fashion craze of the 'zoot suit'. Popular among young African Americans, zoots were wildly exaggerated in size and colours. Over-long jackets, with tails extending to the knees, were combined with billowing thirty-inch trouser legs that narrowed to twelve inches at the ankle. The end product was a suit of tent like pro-portions, topped with a brimmed hat adorned with a feather.

Initially indicating no more than a showy dress sense, zoot suits took on a new meaning when they were outlawed by a wartime cloth conservation order in April 1942. After this date wearing zoots became a way for some African Americans to demonstrate their indifference to the war effort. In New York Malcolm X pointedly wore a zoot suit when reporting to his army draft board in 1943. On the streets zoots became a focus of anger for white ser-vicemen and civilians because of their implicit lack of patriotism. Passions became so inflamed that devotees of the fashion were subjected to violent assaults from white mobs.

In current affairs programmes national radio broke new ground. On 17 December 1941 NBC launched *Freedom's People*, an eight-part series highlighting the contribution of African Americans to different areas of national life. Produced under the auspices of the US Office of Education, the series featured a cross section of celebrities and used black academics as programme consultants.

In a 1942 edition of *America's Town Meeting on the Air* NBC had a black panel discuss the contribution of African Americans to the war effort. In a 1944 broadcast of *People's Platform* CBS had an interracial panel address the question 'Is the South Solving Its Race Problem?'. Although the answer may have seemed obvious the programme was clearly well intentioned.

The Armed Forces Radio Service (AFRS), set up by the War Department, promoted racial unity in its broadcasts to serviceman at home and abroad. The AFRS aired educational programmes and entertainment shows, like *The Mildred Bailey Show* and *Jubilee*, which included black performers.

One objective of such productions was to neutralize enemy prop-aganda. In a radio offensive Nazi presenters like 'Axis Sally' targeted US servicemen in broadcasts that portrayed African Americans as lazy and subhuman. Japan's 'Tokyo Rose' pursued a different line of attack, playing race records and reminding black GIs of racial injustice in the United States. In a counterblast the American Office of War Information's international broadcast network, later to be known as *The Voice of America*, aired pro-grammes in different languages around the world that emphasized the just nature of the allied cause.

Back in United States local radio, WMCA, in New York City, launched *New World a-Coming* in 1944. Only accessible to New Yorkers, the show, hosted by actor Canada Lee, was nonetheless a pioneering initiative, featuring documentaries on racial issues, dramas with black performers, and appearances by African American celebrities.

Sporting competitions were badly hit by the war. Baseball continued but teams were weakened as leading players were drafted. This player shortage gave added momentum to the campaign being waged by black sportswriters and some of their white colleagues for an end to the unwritten ban that prevented black stars from playing major league baseball. Another boost came from the death of Baseball Commissioner, Kennesaw Mountain Landis, in 1944. A strong opponent of integration, Landis had dominated the national organization of the game since his appointment in 1921.

The career of Joe Louis during the 1930s had demonstrated that white audiences could accept black sporting celebrities. During the war Louis consolidated his popularity by donating the proceeds from two defences of his world title to army and navy charities. Enlisted in the army, Louis headed a troupe of African American boxers that fought exhibition bouts at army bases to raise morale.

Elsewhere major international sporting events were abandoned altogether. The 1940 Olympic Games, scheduled to be held in Tokyo, was cancelled, as was the 1944 Olympiad. Count Henri Baillet-Latour's exhortation to 'the youth of every country', at the closing ceremony of the Berlin Games, 'to assemble in four years in Tokyo' took on ironic new meaning.

CHAPTER THREE

The Civil Rights era, 1945–65

Historians often see war as a catalyst for social change. The experience of US race relations in the late 1940s provides partial justification for this viewpoint. The defeat of Nazi Germany and realization of the full horrors of the Holocaust contributed to a discrediting of scientific racism. Some white Americans experienced self-doubt about segregation and discrimination in the United States.

The attitudes of black Americans were also affected. Over 1 million African Americans had enlisted in the US armed forces between 1941 and 1945 and expected better treatment in recognition of their service to the nation. Some 132,000 black Americans had been stationed in the United Kingdom during 1942–4 as part of the build up for the D-Day landings. They contrasted the comparatively enlightened views of the British public on race relations with those of white southerners back home.

In 1946 Harry S. Truman, who became US President following the death of Franklin Roosevelt in April 1945, set up a high-profile independent committee to investigate the state of race relations in the nation. The following year it produced a frank report, *To Secure These Rights*, that highlighted the disturbing extent of racial injustice and called for a wide-ranging series of initiatives to address the problem. In 1948 Truman initiated the desegregation of the US armed forces with his Executive Order 9981.

In the *Brown* v. *Board of Education* case of 1954 the US Supreme Court, in a unanimous decision, ruled that segregation in education was unconstitutional. The most important judicial pronouncement on race relations during the twentieth century, the ruling overturned the pro-segregation 'separate but equal' doctrine laid down by the Supreme Court in the *Plessy* v. *Ferguson* decision of 1896.

Sport reflected the changing national mood. In 1945 African Americans Kenny Washington and Woody Strode signed with the Los Angeles Rams in the National Football League (NFL). The following year two black players, Marion Motley and Bill Willis, turned out for the Cleveland Browns. Also in 1946 William 'Pop' Gates and William 'Dolly' King became the first blacks to play on previously all-white professional basketball teams. In the 1949–50 season black teams were finally allowed to play in the National Basketball Association (NBA) league.

In 1947 Jackie Robinson became the first African American to play in major league baseball, with the Brooklyn Dodgers. This breakthrough paved the way for other black stars, like Don Newcombe and Roy Camponella, to make a career in the major leagues. In 1959, the Boston Red Sox, the last all-white team in major league baseball, accepted the inevitable and signed a black player Elijah 'Pumpsie' Green.

In international competition the pattern was similar. At the 1948 Olympic Games in London, African Americans, like sprinters Harrison Dillard and Norwood Ewell, had a prominent role in the US team. Thereafter black athletes became a regular part of US Olympic squads.

In boxing the story was not so much black participation as black domination. When Joe Louis retired as undefeated World Heavyweight Champion in 1947, fellow African Americans Ezzard Charles, 1949–51, and 'Jersey' Joe Walcott, 1951–2, succeeded him.

In the 1950s a new 'great white hope' 'Rocky' Marciano, wrested the crown from Walcott. Predictably, Marciano became a focus for racist supporters as he bludgeoned black challengers onto the canvas in a series of title defences. Southern segregationists saw him as a symbol of white supremacy in their 'Massive Resistance' to the implementation of the *Brown* ruling.

Such thinking was misplaced. Marciano himself was no racist and his success did not herald a new era of white domination in the sport. Although 'the Rock' retired undefeated in 1956 he was the last white American in the twentieth century to hold the world heavyweight crown.

The same year African American, Floyd Patterson, won the elimination contest to determine Marciano's successor. Although dethroned by a white challenger, Ingemar Johansson, in 1959, Patterson regained and retained the title in two further contests against the Swede in 1960. Patterson's nemesis, in 1962, came against fellow African American, 'Sonny' Liston. Liston in turn held the title until defeated by Cassius Clay in 1964. In 1965 Liston was bested in a rematch, though by this time Clay was fighting under the name of Muhammad Ali.

Some things did not change. In the 1950s it became apparent that former Champion Joe Louis was hopelessly in debt, owing some $1.2 million in back taxes alone. Financial problems forced the ageing Louis out of retirement leading to humiliating defeats against younger fighters, Charles and Marciano. Even more demeaning, in 1956 he took up a career in wrestling.

In part Louis's problems were self-inflicted, a result of extravagant spending and his fondness for gambling. His income was also depleted by tax rises for high earners during the war and early post-war period. At the same time Louis was a victim of the familiar pattern of white exploitation of black talent, with his handlers, John Roxburgh and Mike Jacobs, amassing considerable personal wealth from his success.

The most striking development in US popular culture in the post-war era was the emergence of television. First available in the late 1940s the new medium was initially accessible to only a small minority. In 1949 just 3 per cent of American homes possessed a television set. Despite this it soon became clear that television was the entertainment of the future. By 1951 12 per cent of US homes possessed a set, rising to 24 per cent in 1954, 72 per cent in 1956, and 90 per cent by 1963.

Technologically innovative, the content of early television programming was unimaginative. Just as radio in the 1920s had drawn from minstrelsy, so early television looked to radio for inspiration. The result was the repackaging of old stereotypes in a new format.

Amos 'n' Andy was turned into a television series that ran on CBS from 1951. The one concession to the visual medium was that the lead roles were now taken by two African Americans, with Alvin Childress appearing as Amos and Spencer Williams as Andy. The show reached thirteenth place in the national ratings during the 1951–2 season.

Echoing the earlier 1930s crusade of the *Pittsburgh Courier*, the NAACP launched a campaign against the show. On this occasion the protest was successful. CBS withdrew the programme in 1953, although it continued to play in reruns on other stations until the mid-1960s.

Beulah, another radio creation, was also reborn on television, running on ABC from 1950–3. Chronicling the comic adventures of a black housekeeper, the show marked another reincarnation of the mammy stereotype. Jovial, overweight, and more concerned about the welfare of her white employers than her own family, the Beulah character was designed to have maximum appeal to white audiences.

She was less endearing to the black actresses cast in the role. The first television Beulah, Ethel Waters, gave up the part in 1952, unwilling to star in 'a white folks kitchen comedy'. Briefly replaced by Hattie McDaniel, who died the same year, the lead then fell to Louise Beavers. Also uneasy with the role, Beavers left the show in 1953, and ABC abandoned the programme.

The stand taken by Waters and Beavers was courageous, as the show represented one of the few opportunities for African Americans on early television. Naturally, there were some exceptions. Eddie Anderson reprised his radio role of Rochester on *The Jack Benny Show* from 1950–65, and black celebrities like Louis Armstrong, Cab Calloway and Duke Ellington made guest appearances on programmes like *Tonight* or the *Ed Sullivan Show*. African Americans like Jackie Robinson and Floyd Patterson also featured in the coverage of sporting events.

Such occasions aside, blacks rarely appeared on entertainment programmes before the mid-1960s. Instead, feel-good shows like *Lassie* and *Bewitched* focused on the lives of idyllic white families who inhabited a world in which African Americans didn't exist. During 1952 black actors and actresses accounted for only 0.4 per cent of all performances on television and of the 6,620 actors who appeared on television in an average week just thirty-one were black.

There were several reasons for this exclusion. The birth of television preceded the emergence of the Civil Rights Movement of 1955–68 and the cautious nature of the medium made it slow to adjust to the changes of the period. The reasons for this conservatism were the same as had applied to radio in the interwar period. Most TV viewers were white. In part this was because of simple demography, African Americans comprising only around 12 per cent of the total US population. The imbalance was accentuated by economic inequality, many blacks being unable to afford a television set.

All the major television sponsors represented white-owned companies. These were unwilling to fund programmes with African Americans lest their product become perceived as black-oriented and shunned by white consumers. They were also reluctant to be associated with shows that might cause offence to key market groups like southern whites.

The combined effect of such factors was dramatic. In 1956 *The Nat King Cole Show* was launched as a weekly 15-minute slot by NBC. A popular singer, Cole had a courteous manner and avoided controversy. The show's prospects seemed good but it was withdrawn after just one season, because of problems in finding a sponsor, poor ratings and complaints from whites.

East Side/West Side, which premiered on CBS in 1963, attempted to break with past precedent. Different dramatic presentations each week sought to explore controversial issues, like racism. Although the show coincided with the peak years of the Civil Rights Movement it was still too provocative for its day. Lacking viewers and sponsors the programme was wound up after twenty-four episodes in April 1964.

The most important portrayals of African Americans on television in the 1950s and early 1960s came not on entertainment programmes but in news bulletins and documentaries. Excluded from the make-believe world of light entertainment, the scale of black civil rights protests in these years made them impossible for the television networks to ignore in their coverage of real events.

For the first time northern whites witnessed the violent response of southern white police forces and members of the public to peaceful protests by black demonstrators. Southern police chiefs, who often appeared loutish and uneducated before the television cameras, contrasted unfavourably with the intelligent, reasonable impression created by Martin Luther King and other civil rights leaders. The nature of such images played an important, if unquantifiable, part in mobilizing northern white opinion in support of civil rights.

Another defining moment came with a 1959 documentary, *The Hate That Hate Creates*, which investigated the black separatist organization, the Nation of Islam (NOI). Previously unknown to most white Americans, the Nation was portrayed in the programme as a dangerous hate-whites sect.

NOI minister Malcolm X, who featured prominently in the documentary, became a nationally known figure overnight. He subsequently appeared as a regular contributor in television discussions on racial issues, becoming a voice of inspiration for black militants and a demonic figure for white audiences. Ironically, the disturbing impression created by such interviews may have actually reinforced white support for Martin Luther King, as the voice of moderation, a potential outcome that was appreciated both by Dr King and Malcolm X himself.

The early post-war era was a difficult time for the American film industry. Between 1946 and 1949 profits in Hollywood fell by 45 per cent. The emergence of television created the possibility that Americans would stay at home for their entertainment rather than go to the cinema. Unlike filmmakers of the early twenty-first century, producers and directors of the late 1940s were not able to rely on lavish computer generated special effects to win back audiences. Instead they turned to making adult 'problem' films, examining issues like mental illness and juvenile delinquency that were too controversial for television. It was hoped that the provocative nature of the subject matter would encourage Americans to venture out to the cinema as a change from the saccharine diet available on TV.

Racism was one adult theme to be addressed. *Home of the Brave* (1949) focused on the trauma of a black GI, suffering from partial amnesia and hysterical blindness, and the efforts of a white psychiatrist to treat him. *Intruder in the Dust* (1949), based on the novel of the same name by William Faulkner, portrayed the ordeal of an African American in the South who was wrongly accused of murdering a local white man. Two other films released the same year, *Pinky* and *Lost Boundaries*, fell back on the old theme of the tragic mulatto, relating the doomed attempts of mixed-race characters to pass for white. Ironically, white actors and actresses played the lead roles in both productions.

In 1950 *No Way Out* marked the screen debut of Sidney Poitier. Portraying a hard working hospital doctor subjected to almost intolerable strain and provocation, Poitier played the type of role that was to become his trademark in the 1950s and 1960s. In doing so he contributed to the creation of a new Hollywood stereotype, 'the ebony saint'.

This character was typically well spoken, highly educated, immaculately but conservatively dressed, and always retained his composure, despite intense provocation. Saintliness also had other connotations. The new creation did not drink, smoke, swear or have sexual relationships.

Following his successful debut Poitier went on to enjoy a screen career in the 1950s and 1960s that African American actors of earlier generations could only have dreamed of, making him the first black superstar in Hollywood. In *The Blackboard Jungle* (1955) he played a troubled student in a deprived inner-city school.

In *The Defiant Ones* (1958), he was cast as a convict on the run, manacled to fellow escapee Tony Curtis. The racial bigotry of the white felon at first led to a bad relationship between the two men but, by the end of the film, they became friends. Coinciding with the rise of the civil rights movement, the optimistic message of the film seemed to be that mutual understanding and a willingness to talk things through was all that was needed to resolve the nation's racial problems.

How to exploit Poitier's obvious sex appeal for female cinema-goers without causing offence was a recurring problem for Hollywood filmmakers. The result was a series of contrived story-lines. In *Lilies of the Field* (1963) he played a handyman working for a community of nuns. This made it possible to suggest mutual sexual attraction between Poitier and the white sisters, but at the same time their religious vows made it clear that this would never be consummated. Otherwise forgettable, the film was memorable in that Poitier became the first African American in screen history to receive an Oscar for best actor for his role.

In *The Long Ships* (1964) it was Poitier himself who was subject to religious self-denial. Playing a Moorish pirate, there was obvious sexual chemistry between Poitier and a beautiful white woman hostage. Ravishment or seduction were, however, ruled out, as the brigand had taken an oath of celibacy.

Another variant on a familiar theme came in *A Patch of Blue* (1965). Poitier was cast opposite a blind white girl who developed romantic feelings towards him but, because of her disability, was unaware of his race. Despite a brief screen kiss the relationship never developed to the point of intimacy.

Remarkable though Poitier's career was, opportunities for black Americans in film in the 1950s and early 1960s were limited. Poitier himself summed up the situation when he reflected that 'I knew that we hadn't overcome' in Hollywood since he 'was still the only one'.

Alongside Poitier the actress Dorothy Dandridge was another rising black film star in the 1950s. In common with him she also suffered from stereotyped casting. In Dandridge's case this was the part of the sensual temptress, a role she first played in *Carmen Jones* (1954), a modern version of Bizet's opera *Carmen* set in Chicago and the southern United States during the Second World War.

This was followed by starring roles in *Island in the Sun* (1957) and a film version of *Porgy and Bess* (1959), Dandridge's last major Hollywood role before her suicide in 1965 at the age of forty-two. Cast as Porgy, Poitier co-starred with Dandridge, but only after strong pressure from Hollywood executives to take the part, which he regarded as demeaning. Albeit unsuccessful, Poitier's stance was notable in showing how attitudes had changed since the 1920s, when Paul Robeson's casting in the role had been seen as a break-through for African Americans in the theatre.

A box office success, *Island in the Sun* was controversial, dealing with the theme of interracial love. Dandridge made screen history by becoming the first African American actress to be held in the arms of a white actor in a major film production. In another storyline in the film white actress Joan Fontaine became romantic-ally involved with the black actor and singer Harry Belafonte. Although there was little physical contact between them the mere suggestion of such a relationship was provocative by the film standards of the day.

The decision of director Darryl Zanuck to deal with such a subject reflected both changing attitudes on racial issues in America in the 1950s and a continued willingness of filmmakers to address provocative subjects to attract cinema audiences. These two factors also inspired the less memorable 1964 production *Black Like Me*, a film based on the book of the same name by white journalist John Howard Griffin.

A bestseller in 1960, Griffin's work was a true account of an experiment by the author to investigate race relations in the American South. Taking drugs to turn his skin pigment black, Griffin contrasted the differing treatment accorded to him as a white man and in his guise of an African American. On publication the book was billed as a shocking expose of racism and Griffin was subjected to hate mail and death threats from the South.

Despite this reaction, and Griffin's liberal views on race, the good intentions of the book were undermined by serious weaknesses. Spending only sixty days in the South, and financially independent, Griffin's undercover story did not recreate the life-long experience of poor black sharecroppers in the region. If often shocking and dangerous, the experiment was also a novel adventure that Griffin had the power to end as and when he saw fit.

Moreover, if black on the outside, in his inner consciousness Griffin remained white. When subjected to racial abuse his first response was to reflect on how his tormenters would feel if they knew he was really white, rather than to experience feelings of hurt. In consequence his account, albeit unintentionally, appeared patronizing.

Condescending white attitudes pervaded many Hollywood productions between 1950 and 1965. In a number of films African Americans were cast in token roles to highlight the racial liberalism of directors, producers and fellow actors. The 'rat pack' films of Frank Sinatra, Dean Martin, Peter Lawford, and Sammy Davis Jr. were one example of this genre.

Superficially, productions like *Ocean's Eleven* (1960) and *Robin and the Seven Hoods* (1964) demonstrated the enlightened views of the white leads by their inclusion of Davis in the group. The reality was less uplifting, however, the black entertainer being consigned to the role of a sidekick and the subject of racial jokes. A contrived scene in *Robin and the Seven Hoods* required the cast to disguise themselves in Santa Claus costumes, providing an opportunity to make fun of Davis as a black Father Christmas. Albeit less crude, the 'rat pack' films with Davis evoked memories of the parts played by Stepin Fetchit and Willie Best in the 1930s.

Music, like other areas of popular culture, experienced major changes after the Second World War. By the late 1940s the era of the big bands was over. Solo singers, like Frank Sinatra, who gained public prominence as a result of the wartime ban on recording music, were the new musical celebrities. The post-war economic climate also made it difficult to retain large ensembles. Ballrooms closed, bands lost work and between 1947 and 1949 record sales fell by over $50 million, more than 20 per cent of the total income for the industry.

Swing, the music associated with the big band era, went out of fashion. A fresh generation of African American musicians, led by

Charlie 'Bird' Parker and Dizzy Gillespie, introduced the nation to Bebop, a new style of Jazz that they had pioneered during the war. Progressive or modern Jazz, as the new music was also called, was largely instrumental and highly complex. It was also more distinctively African American in contrast to the mainstream, European style of Swing. Performers like Parker and Gillespie dismissed the traditional or 'trad' Jazz style of pre-war artists like Louis Armstrong as out of date.

Bebop was highly innovative, acclaimed by the critics, and rapturously received by Jazz connoisseurs at chic venues like 'Birdland' in New York City. It also lacked popular appeal. The new music was unsuitable for dancing. Sophisticated and subtle, it could only be fully appreciated by listeners knowledgeable in Jazz traditions. Difficult to play, it could only be performed well by the most able musicians. Moreover, the death of Charlie Parker in March 1955, aged thirty-four, deprived Bebop of its greatest exponent.

Traditional Jazz, though more to the public taste, also declined in popularity. By the end of the 1950s Jazz, once dominant in American popular music, had become a minority interest. In part this was a consequence of the rise of television. People stayed at home for their entertainment rather than going out to nightclubs. More importantly, it was a result of changing musical tastes. In 1945, before the advent of television, Jazz was already being outsold by the new phenomenon of Rhythm and Blues, or R & B as it became known.

First developed in the war by African American musicians like Louis Jordan and Lionel Hampton, R & B was a kind of electrified urban Blues combined with elements of gospel vocal styles and swing instrumental arrangements. Put more simply, it was a way of making the Blues 'jump'. R & B records were lively and easy to dance to. Young black Americans also perceived R & B as being more sophisticated than traditional Blues, which were seen as unrefined, and an unwelcome reminder of the segregated South.

Jazz suffered from the opposite problem of having a middle-class image. This view was reinforced by the complex techniques of Bebop and the fact that a number of leading Jazz performers, like Duke Ellington, were well educated and came from a comparatively privileged background.

A number of factors contributed to the rapid spread of Rhythm and Blues. The new music first developed in the South. During the war black servicemen from the North encountered R&B whilst stationed at military training camps, many of which were located in southern states. Liking what they heard, they took the music with them when they returned home. In another large-scale migration over 1 million black southerners left the region during the 1940s, settling in the North and rapidly growing urban centres on the West Coast, like Los Angeles and San Francisco.

In the record industry the development of magnetic tape after the war, and introduction of high-fidelity 33 rpm and 45 rpm records, were important technological developments that made it easier and cheaper to make records. Between 1945 and 1949 this resulted in the growth of more than 400 new independent labels. Less conservative than the established companies, the new labels were more innovative in their releases, making it easier for R&B artists to secure record contracts.

Recent migrants and returning black servicemen provided a lucrative market for R&B recordings in major cities, which comprised the biggest market for records. Radio disc jockeys began to devote airtime to Rhythm and Blues artists, boosting sales still further. They enabled young white Americans to become familiar with the work of R&B performers like Fats Domino and Lloyd Price.

In the years 1954–6, when the *Brown* decision began the move towards legal desegregation in American society, black R&B artists started to enjoy 'crossover' success, achieving major record sales in the white market. At the same time R&B itself evolved into Rock and Roll. A number of black musicians, like Chuck Berry and Little Richard, became leading Rock and Roll entertainers, but over time white performers became the commercially dominant figures of the new genre.

A recurring pattern emerged in which white vocalists like Pat Boone, Bill Haley and Elvis Presley recorded cover versions of numbers first released by black entertainers. Usually of less artistic merit than the originals, these sold better because they were packaged in a way that was more acceptable to white consumers. The familiar phenomenon of black roots and white fruits was repeated.

Over time the most talented white performers like Presley, Jerry Lee Lewis and Buddy Holly developed a distinctive style of their own. This resulted in a 'whitening' of Rock and Roll music as it moved away from its African American origins and incorporated other influences, most notably country and western music. Rock and Roll was reshaped to meet white tastes just as Jazz had been with the development of Swing in the 1930s.

This process was most evident in the emergence of 'schlock rock' in the early 1960s in which clean cut, conservative, and predominantly white vocalists, like Frankie Avalon, Neil Sedaka and Connie Francis, released sanitized versions of Rock and Roll numbers that were so middle of the road there was little risk of their causing offence. Some black performers like 'Chubby Checker', whose very stage name seemed an imitative variant on 'Fats Domino', also capitalized on the genre. Reworking a recording by an earlier black group, Checker's 1960 release 'The Twist' went on to inspire a new dance craze in the early years of the decade.

The rise of Bebop and Rhythm and Blues reflected a growing sense of racial and cultural pride among young African Americans in the late 1940s. The publication of *Invisible Man* (1952), by Ralph Ellison, was indicative of this trend. Possibly the most influential and widely read novel by an African American in the twentieth century, the work centred on the experiences of the black narrator of the title.

Unhappy at the way African Americans had been portrayed in existing literary texts, Ellison described events like the Great Migration and race riots from a black perspective. The book rejoiced in references to African American life and culture that could only be fully appreciated by black readers. On the bestseller list for sixteen weeks, by 1982 *Invisible Man* had gone through twenty hardback and seventeen paperback editions and been translated into at least fifteen languages.

Radio underwent a process of radical transformation as a result of the rise of television. Once the nation's most popular form of entertainment, from the late 1940s radio audience ratings collapsed. Radio was unable to compete with the visual appeal of television. Moreover, many of the leading performers and shows of the 1930s and 1940s, like *Amos 'n' Andy*, deserted to the new medium, denuding radio networks of their most popular programmes. The decline in listening audiences led to major national sponsors defecting from radio as well. These preferred to advertise their products on one of the four major television networks, NBC, CBS, ABC and Du Mont.

In order to survive these setbacks radio stations were forced to undertake a rethink of their programming strategy. The most obvious development was that the major national networks gave way to large numbers of small, autonomous local stations. This change was the result of a variety of different factors.

Unable to attract national sponsors, radio bosses were forced to look to local advertisers instead. Modest in scale, and unable to afford the high costs of promoting their products on television, these were still willing to pay for advertising time on neighbourhood stations.

Radio programmers were also forced to seek out new listeners to replace their lost audiences. One way of doing this was to develop community-based broadcasting, reporting on local news and events, providing a service that TV, with its more national orientation, was less able to cater for. In the same vein radio stations sought to appeal to minority and specialist audiences, whose needs were not met by television.

An important consequence of these strategies was the emergence of black-appeal radio. Largely ignored by the major networks during the golden era of radio in the 1930s, stations now began to seek out black listeners. The reasons for this were commercial rather than a result of more enlightened thinking. The continued migration of African Americans to urban centres in the north and on the west coast meant that many cities in the United States had a large black population living within a small geographical area. This made them an ideal target audience for local radio stations with a limited broadcasting radius.

Moreover, black Americans were one of the groups most likely to be won over by radio. In the late 1940s many African Americans were unable to afford the cost of purchasing a television set, but over 90 per cent of urban blacks, and 70 per cent of blacks in rural districts, had access to radio. Television entertainment programmes, filled with images of wholesome white families and presenters, also offered little to attract black viewers.

Although African Americans earned on average only 60 per cent of the wages of white workers in 1950, their spending power still made them important to radio programmers. In 1948 the total annual spending power of black Americans amounted to some $10,000,000,000, rising to $15,000,000,000 in 1952 and $27,000,000,000 by 1963. In many districts African Americans made up the majority of consumers, making local businesses that advertised on radio dependent on black custom.

In 1948, the year that national network television was launched, WDIA in Memphis, Tennessee, a city with a 40 per cent black population, became the first radio station to capitalize on the importance of African American listeners. Moving to a black-appeal format the station's white owners, John Pepper and Bert Ferguson, consciously targeted black audiences. By 1949 WDIA had risen from last to first place in the local radio ratings with an audience share of 28 per cent. The net profits of the station rose from under $2,000 in 1948 to $100,000 in 1957, when Pepper and Ferguson sold the station for $1 million.

Other radio stations across the nation heeded the message. In 1949 there were four radio stations in the United States with black-appeal formats. This rose to over 200 by 1954 and some 400 by 1956.

An obvious prerequisite of black-appeal radio was the hiring of more black presenters. Also important was the move to a disc jockey format. This was not only inexpensive, but allowed stations to win over black listeners by playing the new R & B records which were shunned by television and more conservative radio stations.

Black disc jockeys playing music by Rhythm and Blues artists became increasingly common across the United States during the 1950s. To give themselves a distinctive airtime identity they often adopted a flamboyant persona, with broadcasting names like 'Daddie O' Daylie' in Chicago, 'Doctor Hep Cat' in Austin, Texas, and 'Jocko Henderson' and 'Lord Fauntleroy', both in Philadelphia.

In contrast to earlier black radio presenters, who had adopted the style of white announcers, the new DJs emphasized their African American identity. They discussed issues of interest to black listeners. In a style pioneered by presenter Al Benson in Chicago, black DJs spoke in 'jive talk', streetwise language and pronunciation that comprised the daily speech of black communities. Commonly known as 'rhyming and signifying', this involved speaking in rhyming sentences and engaging in verbal banter using ghetto slang. A means of conveying information in a way that made it incomprehensible to most whites, the practice had its origins in the speech patterns of ante-bellum slaves.

A significant breakthrough in meeting the needs and interests of African American communities, black-appeal radio was less radical than it appeared. Although it gave black presenters unprecedented airtime black-appeal stations continued to be white owned. In 1956 only three radio stations in the United States were black run. On other black-appeal stations white backers took almost all the profits whilst black presenters had to content themselves with modest salaries. The large majority of non-broadcasting staff, managers and radio technicians, were also white, as were the bulk of advertising sponsors.

In the 1950s white 'crossover' DJs began to take advantage of the popularity of black presenters. In what historian William Barlow has described as 'racial ventriloquy', white broadcasters like 'John R.' Richbourg in Nashville, Tennessee, Alan 'Moondog' Freed in Cleveland, Ohio, and Robert 'Wolfman' Jack, broadcasting into the United States from Mexico, adopted African American speaking styles. Well versed in African American culture, and playing R & B records, they consciously developed a black style persona. A successful ploy in building up a loyal following of both black and white listeners, the practice was in some ways reminiscent of the minstrelsy of an earlier era and the *Amos 'n' Andy* dialogues of Gosden and Correll during the 1920s and 1930s.

In the years 1945–65 developments in US popular culture reflected wider changes in race relations taking place across the nation. Some black entertainers, like Harry Belafonte and comedian Dick Gregory, gave enthusiastic backing to the early civil rights movement, but the best-known celebrity backers of the cause were white entertainers like Bob Dylan and Joan Baez. Ironically, although they sang political songs highlighting racial issues, the folk style of Dylan and Baez had little appeal for black record buyers.

Most black celebrities in show business and sport were initially unenthusiastic when it came to openly supporting civil rights protests. In the case of some, like Jesse Owens, this could be explained by their conservative social and political views. During the 1950s Owens continued to campaign for the Republican administrations of Dwight D. Eisenhower, despite 'Ike's' unwillingness to publicly endorse the 1954 *Brown* ruling.

There were other factors that encouraged non-involvement. An obvious fear, and one played up by white business managers, was that a public stance on a controversial issue would be harmful to career prospects. Outspoken black actors and actresses might find it difficult to gain parts, or be shunned by white audiences at the box office. Crossover R & B performers, dependent on white customers, might suffer a fall in record sales.

Another concern was the risk of official persecution. In the late 1940s and early 1950s, the height of the 'red scare', entertainers, white and black, with actual or perceived left-wing political views, saw their careers ruined.

A socialist and public sympathizer of the Soviet Union, the singer and actor Paul Robeson found it impossible to obtain work in the United States. In 1950 his passport was revoked, preventing him from finding work elsewhere, and he was denied entry into Canada, even though officially no travel documentation was needed for such a visit.

The African American singer and dancer, Josephine Baker, became another victim of persecution, despite the fact that she was by now a French rather than an American citizen. Her public stand against racial injustice attracted unwelcome attention from both the Federal Bureau of Investigation (FBI) and the US State Department. In the early 1950s US Embassy staff in the Caribbean and Latin America did their best to sabotage tours by Baker in the region.

A communications problem of a different sort was that black celebrities did not always find it easy to engage in dialogue with conservative, middle-class organizers of civil rights protests. The psychedelic lifestyle associated with Rock and Roll stars did not blend in well with the Baptist values of church ministers who often led civil rights campaigns. On their part black clergymen were initially unwilling to seek such celebrity support, lest the movement suffer by association. Martin Luther King, old fashioned when it came to popular culture, urged teenagers to abandon Rock and Roll for Gospel music in the advice columns that he wrote for black journals and newspapers.

Despite such unpromising beginnings, over time increasing numbers of black celebrities allied themselves with the civil rights struggle. In part this reflected the success of the movement in changing social attitudes. By the early 1960s the issue of civil rights had acquired mainstream respectability. US Presidents John F. Kennedy and Lyndon Johnson publicly endorsed the cause. In this climate there was less risk for black sportsmen and entertainers in supporting civil rights. There was even a danger that their careers might suffer if they did not voice their commitment to the cause.

The civil rights movement itself was also changing. The formation of the biracial Student Non-violent Coordinating Committee (SNCC) in 1960 was a sign of growing involvement by younger activists. The emergence of spokespersons, like John Lewis and Stokely Carmichael, made the movement more appealing for black musical celebrities.

In 1963 black Jazz legend John Coltrane wrote 'Alabama', a musical elegy for four young girls killed in the state when a black church in the city of Birmingham was bombed by white supremacists. 'Mississippi Goddam', released by African American vocalist Nina Simone in 1963, typified the changing mood. During the course of the 1964 SNCC inspired Summer Project in Mississippi, the song replaced the religious and less radical 'We Shall Overcome' as the unofficial anthem of the civil rights movement.

On the radio black DJs like 'Jockey' Jack Gibson in Atlanta, Paul White in Birmingham, 'Jocko' Henderson in New York City, and Wesley South in Chicago, developed informal links with civil rights organizations. They provided a radio 'grapevine' that enabled civil rights leaders to pass on information and kept local communities informed of civil rights meetings. Based in Cuba, the African American Robert Williams broadcast his radical views on race relations to listeners in the southern United States between 1961 and 1964 in his weekly programme *Radio Free Dixie*.

By the late 1950s the growing momentum of the civil rights movement made even older and more cautious black entertainers feel the need to show their support. On 22 February 1960 Duke Ellington had himself escorted into the Blue Jay restaurant in Baltimore when he learned that black student campaigners had been refused service there. When Ellington was turned away the incident resulted in national press coverage.

During the 1957 Little Rock crisis in Arkansas Louis Armstrong used a press interview to voice his anger at the exclusion of black pupils from the city's high school. He called Arkansas Governor, Orval Faubus, 'a plow boy', and denounced President Eisenhower as 'two faced' and having 'no guts' because of his reluctance to intervene. Satchmo's outburst had added impact in that he was not known for being outspoken, and had toured the globe as a goodwill ambassador for the United States during the 1950s. In calmer vein, Armstrong later made public his thoughts on civil rights in a 1961 article, 'Daddy, How the Country has Changed', for the black journal *Ebony*.

The case of Armstrong highlighted the fact that it was difficult for black entertainers to remain silent on racial issues. It was inevitable that interviewers would ask public figures for their views on news stories about civil rights. Tactful evasion risked giving the impression of moral cowardice, and there was no guarantee that it would be enough to satisfy white conservatives.

Despite having a reputation for being polite and deferential, Nat King Cole was attacked by three white segregationists while performing on stage at the Municipal Auditorium in Birmingham, Alabama, on 10 April 1956. Formerly quiet on racial issues, Cole, perhaps influenced by the incident, subsequently became a committed supporter of the civil rights movement.

Throughout the South white conservatives condemned Rock and Roll music in the late 1950s as part of the 'Massive Resistance' to desegregation that followed the *Brown* decision. The African American associations with the new music resulted in it being denounced as immoral, obscene and injurious to mental health. In 1956 state governments and city councils across the South banned Rock and Roll concerts. If performances did take place there was danger of racial violence, as segregationist demonstrators became incensed at the sight of black entertainers playing to excited white teenagers.

In the nation as a whole conservative opinion formers expressed shock and concern at Rock and Roll, including those who ought to have known better. In 1958 Frank Sinatra dismissed it as 'the most brutal, ugly, degenerate, vicious form of expression' that it had been his 'misfortune to hear'. It was 'phoney and false' and fostered 'almost totally negative and destructive reactions in young people'. Rock and Roll performers were 'for the most part' 'cretinous goons' who composed songs with 'almost imbecilic reiterations and sly-lewd – in plain fact, dirty – lyrics' that amounted to a 'rancid aphrodisiac'.

Sinatra's views demonstrated that it was not just black performers but also white Rock and Roll artists, like Elvis Presley, who were subject to attack. Presley's tight trousers and swivelling hip movements were denounced as likely to promote physical deformity. On television Presley's gyrations were concealed from the public eye lest viewers be offended, or teenagers inflict injury on themselves by trying to imitate his movements.

On radio DJs became a target of attack during the 1960 payola hearings in the US House of Representatives. Payola was the name used to describe the practice of record companies in giving DJs hospitality and/or cash payments to encourage the playing of records on air. Not actually illegal, the custom was condemned in the hearings as corrupt.

Although there was some justification for this view, the vehemence of the charges reflected the fact that payola was a convenient way for conservative critics to introduce restrictions on the playing of music on the radio. Many DJs, like Alan 'Moondog' Freed, lost their jobs in the wake of the hearings. Those that survived lost the freedom to chose the records that they played on air. Instead official Top Forty lists were compiled and DJs had to play tracks selected from these, the number of plays per week being determined by the position of a release in the rankings.

The teenage fans of Rock and Roll were part of a familiar pattern in US race relations. Young white Americans of the 1920s who embraced Jazz did so in part because of the stereotyped views they held of African Americans associated with it. The music, like the black artists who played it, was perceived as being spontaneous and having natural primal rhythm.

In the late 1940s and early 1950s poets of the Beat generation, like Allen Ginsberg, who admired Bebop saw it as improvised and uninhibited, 'a fountain of instantaneous inspiration'. In reality Bebop was so difficult and complex that it was impossible to make up on the spot. White aficionados chose to believe otherwise because of their preconceived notions that these were the qualities associated with black musicians.

Similarly, one of the attractions of black Rock and Roll artists for young whites in the late 1950s and early 1960s was that they were seen as having natural rhythm and were free and open in the expression of their feelings. Even when being admired black entertainers had to tolerate stereotyped perceptions of themselves from white audiences.

CHAPTER FOUR

Black Power, 1965–76

In the late 1960s America was a country at unease with itself. In 1965 peace protesters organized the first concerted demonstrations against the Vietnam War. By 1968 opinion polls showed that the majority of Americans were against the conflict. Racial confrontations spread outside the South. In the 'five long hot summers' of 1964–8 there were serious urban disorders in some 200 American cities, most of which were in the North or on the West Coast.

Violence became a part of political life. Following the assassination of John F. Kennedy, on 22 November 1963, the President's brother, Robert, was killed in 1967, whilst himself campaigning for the Presidency. African Americans also suffered the loss of martyred leaders. On 21 February 1965 Malcolm X was gunned down in Harlem, New York. On 4 April 1968 Martin Luther King was assassinated in Memphis, Tennessee.

The troubled times created problems for television programmers and Hollywood filmmakers. The conservative instincts of decision makers in both industries were offset by the need to keep up with changing public opinion. *The Green Berets*, a 1967 Hollywood production, demonstrated the cost of the failure to adapt. A patriotic defence of the Vietnam War inspired by actor John Wayne, the film flopped at the box office.

The leading cinema attractions for US audiences in 1967 involved more sobering portrayals of social and racial problems. *To Sir With Love* starred Sidney Poitier working as an educator in a deprived inner-city school. A calculated attempt to repeat the success of *The Blackboard Jungle*, the film reworked the plot of the earlier production by casting Poitier as a teacher rather than a student, and moving the setting from the United States to London.

Poitier enjoyed another 1967 triumph with *In the Heat of the Night*. Playing a New York detective, Virgil Tibbs, Poitier's character became involved in a murder case in a small southern town whilst on a family visit in the region. Initially suspected of the killing himself, Tibbs not only proved his innocence but also identified the true culprit, working in an uneasy alliance with the bigoted local police chief played by Rod Steiger. Tense and fast moving, the film highlighted the South's racial problems.

At the same time, *In the Heat of the Night* was less radical than it seemed. References to Tibbs' well-adjusted life in the North gave the impression that race could still be seen as a southern rather than a national problem. The role of the black detective was a reprisal of the 'ebony saint' stereotype that Poitier had played in the 1950s. Intellectual, self-controlled, non-violent, and able to understand and forgive the failings of his tormentors, the character embodied an idealized white vision of black civil rights campaigners as personified by Martin Luther King. Travelling alone in the South, Tibbs conveniently had no love interest, constituting another example of the desexualized black hero.

Guess Who's Coming to Dinner, Poitier's third box office hit of 1967, suffered from similar failings. Portraying an interracial relationship between a world famous doctor John Prentice, played by Poitier, and the white daughter of a white newspaper editor, the film initially appeared ground breaking and provocative. Angry and emotional confrontations between Poitier and his fiancée's parents, played by Katharine Hepburn and Spencer Tracey, highlighted the unspoken racial fears and prejudices harboured even by liberal whites.

The seemingly radical message of the film was, however, diluted to minimize the risk of causing offence. Poitier's Nobel Prize winning character was such a paragon of virtue that it was difficult for anyone to object to him as a potential son-in-law just because of his race. African American playwright Clifford Mason summed up the character as a 'showcase nigger', with a 'clean suit' and a 'complete purity of motivation' that created the appearance of a 'mistreated puppy' with 'all the sympathy on his side'.

Moreover, in their scenes together the star-crossed lovers showed remarkable capacity for self-restraint given the supposedly passionate nature of their relationship. The height of their intimacy came in just one screen kiss, and even this was presented in indirect form. Cinema audiences witnessed the tender moment as a reflection in the rearview mirror of a taxicab in which the couple were travelling.

The fact that Poitier starred in three of the most successful films of 1967 was testimony to his acting ability. Less happily, it demonstrated the career barriers still facing black actors. Entertainers like Harry Belafonte and Sammy Davis Jr. still appeared in Hollywood productions, and African American football star Jim Brown demonstrated talent of a different sort in films like *The Dirty Dozen* (1967) and *Ice Station Zebra* (1968). Nonetheless, despite such successes, Poitier continued to be the only black American film actor with superstar status.

Like their Hollywood counterparts, television programmers struggled to combine conservative instincts with the need to reflect social change. *I Spy* (1965–8) on NBC typified this uneasy compromise. The series focused on the adventures of two government agents, one black and one white, played by Bill Cosby and Robert Culp respectively. In an improbable pairing Cosby's character was a Harvard graduate whilst Culp portrayed an ex-professional tennis player with limited education. In terms of romantic interest it became clear that it was sporting prowess rather than academic ability that mattered. Culp enjoyed a succession of female admirers in the course of the duo's adventures whilst Cosby gave the impression of having taken a vow of celibacy.

Notwithstanding their differing personal backgrounds, the two agents bonded together in an almost brotherly relationship. Seeking to convey an uplifting impression of interracial harmony, the programme dealt with racial issues by refusing to acknowledge their existence. Race simply never came up as a topic of discussion between the two co-stars. The agent played by Cosby was removed from African American culture and society.

In a careful marketing ploy the first nine episodes of the series were set in foreign countries. In part exotic locations reflected a need for glamour that was demanded of any self-respecting spy in film or television. At the same time, such settings avoided the problem of dealing with the issue of segregated accommodations on public transport, and in hotels and restaurants, when the agents travelled together within the United States.

The critical and commercial success of *I Spy* encouraged the development of more television programmes with African American characters. 1966–7 was dubbed the 'Year of the Negro', because of the number of roles given to blacks in series that premiered in that period.

In *Daktari* (1966–9), Hari Rhodes played a native trainee vet in Africa. The name of the programme was taken from the Swahili word for doctor. Less originally, the head of the veterinary practice to which Rhodes was attached was a white American. Once again the role of leadership, even in Africa, was reserved for a white character.

In the action adventure programme *Mission Impossible* (1966–73), Greg Morris played black electronics expert, Barney Coleman. In *Star Trek* (1966–9), Nichelle Nichols played Lieutenant Uhura, an African American communications officer on the bridge of the Starship *Enterprise*. Symbolically, the name Uhura was derived from the word for freedom in Swahili.

Proving that outer space provided hitherto unimagined career opportunities for African Americans, Don Marshall played an aircraft co-pilot in another science fiction series *Land of the Giants* (1969–71). Back on earth, Don Mitchell appeared as a black aide to a disabled white Chief of Police played by Raymond Burr in *Ironside* (1967–75).

In another departure, the *Star Trek* episode *Plato's Stepchildren* reputedly featured the first interracial kiss on television between Lieutenant Uhura and Captain James T. Kirk, played by William Shatner. The moment of passion reflected the fact that unlike earlier portrayals of black women on television, such as Beulah, the character played by Nichols was young and attractive.

The wrangling involved in filming the scene revealed the extraordinary angst of television executives over the potential impact that it might have on audiences and sponsors. An alternative version of the storyline was shot in which the kiss was omitted, to allow final decision on airing to be left to the last possible moment. The plot of the episode made it clear that both Kirk and Uhura had been subjected to mind control by aliens who were compelling them to be intimate. However, in an act of obvious titillation, viewers were made aware that the Captain and his Lieutenant had succeeded in blocking the telepathic powers of their tormenters, yet had to still feign compliance until the right moment presented itself.

The NBC comedy series *Julia* (1968–71) marked a seemingly more straightforward breakthrough. Created by liberal white producer Hal Cantor, the programme featured black actress Diahann Carroll in the title role as a nurse and mother. In its first year on air the show reached seventh spot in the national ratings and at its peak of popularity was watched in some 14 million US homes every week.

Like Uhura, Julia was young, attractive and at ease with white friends and colleagues. Unlike Beulah she was slim, educated and carefully balanced the demands of her job with caring for her child. A significant improvement on earlier portrayals of African American women on television the role of Julia still had limitations. She lived in an all-white neighbourhood far removed from the troubled inner-city black ghettos that featured in nightly news reports. The only African American male in her life was her young son, the husband and father of the family having made the ultimate sacrifice for his country in Vietnam. The character of Julia was attacked by some critics as an 'oriole cookie', a sugary and unhealthy American confection that was black on the outside but white on the inside. Carroll's personal misgivings about the role led her to give up the part, after which NBC abandoned the show.

Significant developments occurred in the music industry in the mid to late 1960s. These reflected a growing sense of racial pride among black Americans that culminated in the emergence of the Black Power movement in the latter half of the decade. Keen to identify with their African American roots black record buyers lost interest in white dominated Rock and Roll music. Soul became the form of popular music most listened to by black Americans. Drawing on the rhythmic and vocal traditions of black gospel music the lyrics of Soul recordings were devoid of religious content. The mix proved ideal in meeting the needs of young African Americans, combining ethnic authenticity with the secular values of the day. Founded by the black entrepreneur Berry Gordy in 1959 the leading Soul record label, Tamla Motown, went on to achieve a peak of commercial success in the years 1964–7.

At the same time, within the civil rights movement a new generation of student activists in the SNCC and Congress of Racial Equality (CORE) became tired of the religiosity and authoritarian style of leadership of older church spokesmen like Martin Luther King. They demanded more democratic forms of decision-making within civil rights organizations, greater emphasis on cultural issues, and international links with black nations in the Third World.

Sensitive to such developments, Soul artists showed increasing racial awareness in their recordings. A genuine desire to express racial ideals combined with hard-headed commercialism as musicians tried to outdo each other in meeting the needs of young black consumers. In 1967 'R-E-S-P-E-C-T', by 'Queen of Soul' Aretha Franklin, became a symbol of racial pride in African American communities. 'Grandfather of Soul', James Brown expressed similar sentiments in songs like 'Soul Pride' and his 1968 release, 'Say It Loud, I'm Black and I'm Proud'.

Supporting words with action Brown publicly backed fundraising and voter registration campaigns launched by the SNCC and the Southern Christian Leadership Conference (SCLC). He toured inner-city districts and organized Operation Black Pride to provide free Christmas meals for ghetto residents in New York City in 1968. At the same time, Brown remained an economic conservative who favoured the idea of black capitalism over charitable disbursements. It also seemed more than just fortunate timing that Brown's Christmas largesse coincided with the release of his latest single, 'Santa Go Straight to the Ghetto', and his *Soulful Christmas* album.

Other voices were more militant. Articulating the frustrations of ghetto communities, Soul group Sly and the Family Stone released an album 'There's A Riot Going On' (1971) that constituted a sustained attack on American values. The politically aware poet and musician Gil Scott-Heron warned listeners of possible future developments with songs like 'The Revolution Will Not Be Televised' and the prophetic 'Winter In America'.

By the early 1970s many artists expressed disillusionment at the continued failure of American society to overcome racial and economic injustice, but not all were bleak in outlook. Stevie Wonder's 'Heaven Help Us All' highlighted the ills of American society but held out the hope that these could yet be overcome. In a series of albums in the early 1970s, *Where I'm Coming From, Music of My Mind, Talking Book, Innervisions, Fulfillingness First Finale* and *Songs in the Key of Life,* Wonder examined contemporary social and political problems in more detail. If at times plaintive and despairing, he still appeared to retain his faith in the power of love and human understanding to prevail. Similarly, Marvin Gaye's 1971 album, *What's Going On,* if troubled by developments not just in America but around the world, also offered the hope of ultimate redemption.

Less uplifting were the sexist attitudes that became increasingly prevalent in the work of Soul artists by the late 1960s. Soul musicians, most notably James Brown, in common with earlier Rhythm and Blues performers had always demonstrated elements of political incorrectness in their attitudes towards women. This tendency became more overt by the end of the decade.

In part this was a consequence of greater public openness about sexual relations. Less happily, it reflected the male chauvinism of the Black Power Movement. Male black leaders in organizations like SNCC, CORE and the revolutionary Black Panthers saw women less as co-workers than objects of sexual gratification. Similarly, Soul recordings increasingly portrayed women as sex objects and evoked images of male sexual potency.

In a wider context this development represented the re-emergence of what historian Robin Kelley has described as 'a long and ignoble tradition' of misogyny and aggressive sexism in the popular music of male African American artists. Historically, the manifestation and intensity of such sentiments have followed a cyclical pattern. In the early years of the twentieth century, when African American communities were subjected to economic deprivation and intense segregation and discrimination, male Blues singers found self-esteem by boasting of their sexual prowess and asserting their dominance over women.

During the late 1950s and early 1960s desegregation and advances in race relations were accompanied by less overtly macho sentiments in the lyrics of Rhythm and Blues performers. Sexual boasting and suggestive language did not disappear, but they became less common. Songs tended to become more romanticized in tone, evoking images of mutual love and respect between the sexes.

In the late 1960s the mounting despair of black Americans at the failure to overcome economic, social and racial problems was accompanied by a resurgence of sexist attitudes in Soul lyrics. Ironically, at the same time that African Americans were losing faith in the possibility of integration, Soul artists, like R & B performers before them, were achieving crossover success with white consumers. Up to 75 per cent of the sales of nationally successful Soul releases went to white record buyers.

Like Soul artists, some black Jazz musicians also incorporated changing racial attitudes into their work. Practitioners of 'New Jazz', or 'Free Jazz' as it was also known, like Ornette Coleman,

John Coltrane and Charlie Mingus, abandoned western ideas of harmony in their work. Instead they sought to rediscover African American rhythm and improvization. In this instance political idealism did not go hand in hand with commercial success. New Jazz albums, in common with other Jazz releases, failed to achieve good record sales.

In an attempt to make their music more popular other Jazz artists, like Miles Davis, sought to develop a new style of 'Fusion', combining Jazz melodies with elements of Rock. At first such hybrid releases did well, Davis's 1969 album *Bitches Brew* selling over 400,000 copies within a year, but the success did not last. Fusion records were viewed as artistic betrayals by Jazz aficionados and were unable to fully satisfy Rock and Roll fans either.

In the mid-1970s Davis gave up playing Jazz altogether, labelling it the 'music of the museum'. During the late 1930s Swing had accounted for 70 per cent of the profits of record companies. By 1975 Jazz releases in all its forms comprised less than 3 per cent of profits in the industry. The death of Louis Armstrong in 1971, and Duke Ellington in 1974, provided symbolic confirmation that the golden age of Jazz had passed. Still drawing artistic inspiration from its black roots, Jazz continued to be a unique form of American cultural expression. Sadly, it was no longer popular.

Located in the communities that they broadcasted to, black radio DJs often had first hand experience of the violent urban disorders of the late 1960s, most commonly taking on the role of peacemakers. In 1964 Jocko Henderson appealed to ghetto rioters for calm in New York and Philadelphia, aided in the latter instance by fellow DJ Georgie Woods. Martha Jean 'The Queen' Steinberg acted as a pacifier in the 1967 Detroit riot. Across the nation black DJs appealed to African American communities for calm in the aftermath of the assassination of Martin Luther King in 1968.

Such community service received little recognition from police forces and city authorities that preferred to take the credit themselves for restoring order. Nathanial 'The Magnificent' Montague, the leading black DJ in Los Angeles, was even more unfortunate. Known for the catchphrase 'Burn, Baby, Burn', his slogan took on new meaning when rioters in the Watts district of the city took it up, in August 1965. Montague was blamed for inciting the disorder and lost his job on radio.

The growth of black consciousness in the late 1960s resulted in the continued rise of black-appeal radio, with some 310 stations adopting this format by 1970. Moving with the times, DJs now played mainly Soul music rather than Rhythm and Blues or Rock and Roll. Generally, black-appeal stations devoted around 70 per cent of their airtime to playing music, 20 per cent to religious topics, and only 5 per cent to news and public affairs. Although black-appeal radio did reflect the needs and interests of local communities, broadcasting centred on providing entertainment rather than discussing controversial issues.

At the end of the 1960s the overwhelming majority of radio stations, even those with a black-appeal format, continued to be white-owned and managed. In 1970 just sixteen of the 8,000 radio outlets in the nation were black-run. Most sponsors were also white. Inevitably there were some black successes. Two African American radio networks, the Mutual Black Network (MBM) and the National Black Network (NBN) were founded in 1972 and 1973 respectively. Generally, however, the statistics confirmed the continuing lack of black economic empowerment in the industry.

The significance of this imbalance should not be exaggerated. Some white station owners were sympathetic on civil rights issues. Conversely, the three stations owned by James Brown were used principally to bankroll the Soul star's lavish personal lifestyle rather than to further racial ideals.

Almost all station owners, black or white, were motivated primarily by commercial considerations. Any that were not were unlikely to remain in business. It was this money making instinct, coupled with the tastes of radio listeners, rather than bias on the part of white owners and managers, that accounted for the limited amount of time devoted to political issues on black-appeal stations.

Black radio presenters of the late 1960s and early 1970s were still badly underpaid, generally receiving less than half the salaries paid to their white counterparts. The introduction of a 'Top Forty' Soul chart meant that black DJs, like white presenters, lost control over which records they played on air, a development that con- tributed to the decline of personality DJs.

In 1965–6 the desire to improve working conditions for African Americans in the industry led to a power struggle in the black-run National Association of Radio Announcers (NARA). In elections at the union's 1965 annual convention a group of young militants, the 'New Breed', ousted older spokesmen from office.

In 1966–7 the new leadership, headed by Del Shields, changed the name of the organization to the National Association of Television and Radio Announcers (NATRA) and issued a series of demands. These included more black ownership of radio stations, the creation of a black news service and more employment opportunities for African American broadcasters. To this end it was proposed that a professional training college be established for black recruits to the industry.

The initiatives failed. New Breed spokesmen were bedevilled by the same problems that beset black activists across the nation. Ambitious in their goals, union organizers lacked the economic resources to turn their aspirations into reality. Alarmed by the radicalism of the new leadership, white sponsors withheld funding. NATRA suffered from internal dissension over the future direction the organization should take. By the mid-1970s the issue was irrelevant. The union collapsed as a result of financial problems and internecine feuding.

Black sportsmen took a prominent public role in the troubles of the late 1960s. Initially welcomed as an alternative to the louche Sonny Liston, new World Heavyweight Boxing Champion Cassius Clay soon became a subject of controversy.

Shortly after winning the title he announced his conversion to the Nation of Islam and took the name Muhammad Ali. Knowing little about the NOI, most whites perceived it as an extremist organization, not least because of the 1959 television documentary, *The Hate That Hate Creates*. Ali's public image suffered as a result.

Worse followed. Refusal to accept military service, except in the case of a Holy War or Jihad, was a key tenet of NOI theology. This resulted in a personal crisis for Ali when he received an army draft order for the Vietnam War. Despite strong public pressure to conform, and suggestions of a behind the scenes deal that would enable him to fulfil his military service in a non-combat role, the Champion stood by his principles. On 28 April 1967 he formally refused to be inducted into the armed forces.

Within hours the New York Athletic Commission revoked Ali's license to box in the state and declared his world title to be forfeit. All other states followed suit, making it impossible for Ali to fight in the United States. Other countries, like the United Kingdom, continued to recognize Ali as Champion, but the possibility of an overseas defence of his title was removed when the US authorities confiscated his passport. The world boxing organizations staged an elimination contest to find a replacement titleholder, culminating in the emergence of a new Champion, Joe Frazier, in 1970.

Denied the means to earn a living in his chosen profession, Ali also faced the possibility of a five-year jail sentence for draft evasion. A prolonged legal battle ensued, with the courts at first upholding, and then denying, his status as a conscientious objector. The issue was finally resolved on 28 June 1971 when the United States Supreme Court ruled that he was not liable to a prison sentence. Deeply divided on the case, the justices used a legal technicality to end their deadlock and reach a decision.

Developments outside the Court contributed to this diplomatic resolution. By 1971 a clear majority of Americans were opposed to the Vietnam War. Many viewed Ali not as a draft dodger but as a courageous individual who had been subjected to legal persecution because of his beliefs. African Americans in particular were outraged at the treatment that he had received, and the pretexts used by the boxing authorities to take away his title.

In November 1967 this anger was a key factor in the launching of a movement by black athletes to boycott the 1968 Olympic Games in Mexico City. Led by Harry Edwards, a black assistant professor in Sociology, the boycott committee launched an 'Olympic Project for Human Rights' outlining its objectives.

The top priority in the manifesto was that Muhammad Ali should have his title and right to box restored. Other demands included the removal of the conservative Avery Brundage as Chairman of the IOC and the exclusion of the apartheid state of South Africa from Olympic competition. Furthermore, the Project called for the appointment of two additional black coaches on the US Olympic team, the appointment of at least two blacks to policy-making positions on the US Olympic Committee, and the desegregation of the New York Athletic Club.

On 20 April 1968 the boycott campaign achieved its first breakthrough when the IOC expelled South Africa from the Olympic movement. A key factor in the decision was a threatened withdrawal from the Games by black African countries, like Ethiopia and Algeria, if South Africa was allowed to take part.

Lacking the support of such powerful allies, other demands of the Olympic Project were not met. Moreover, black athletics selected for the US Olympic team were divided on the boycott movement. Some supported non-participation, but others felt alternative forms of protest would be more effective.

In an effort to maintain unity the call for a boycott was abandoned. Instead, black American athletes at the Games were left to demonstrate their support for the Olympic Project in the way they deemed most appropriate. In a recurring phenomenon of the Black Power era the targeting of far-reaching objectives proved overly ambitious. Advocates of the campaign lacked the necessary means to realize their goals and were unable to command the support of less radical members of the black athletic community.

In Mexico a number of black athletes demonstrated their continued support for the protest in scaled down form. Sprinters Tommie Smith and John Carlos, gold and bronze medal winners respectively in the 200 metres, attended their medal awards ceremony shoeless and dressed in black knee-length stockings. When the US national anthem was played they bowed their heads and, each wearing a black glove, gave a clenched fist Black Power salute. US team managers condemned the action and brought in Olympic legend Jesse Owens to persuade the athletes to apologize for their conduct. They refused and were expelled from the Olympic village.

Intended as a warning to other athletes, this hard-line response had mixed results. Most black US competitors chose to keep their political views to themselves. Others did not. The three African American medallists in the 400-metres relay each attended their medal ceremony wearing a black beret, as did the black American members of the 1,600-metres relay. Long-jumpers Bob Beamon and Ralph Boston each stood shoeless and wearing black socks to receive their medals.

After the Games Jesse Owens and black athletes supporting the protests publicly clashed in strongly worded mutual recriminations. In a 1970 book, *Blackthink*, co-authored with Paul Newark, Owens condemned Black Power advocates as being negative in outlook and guilty of reverse racism. Two years later his views had mellowed. In another book, *I Have Changed*, also co-authored with Newark, Owens showed greater sympathy for black protesters.

By this time the controversy had subsided. At the 1972 Olympics in Munich two more black sprinters, Vincent Matthews and Wayne Collett, were expelled from the Games. Gold and silver medallists respectively, in the 400 metres, the two athletes turned their backs on the American flag when the US national anthem was played at their medal awards ceremony, but there were no other such incidents. By 1972 the protest movement had all but expired. The mood of the Games was also influenced by the murder of Israeli athletes in the Olympic village by Arab terrorists.

In the United States the 1968 Mexico City protests were accompanied by a series of some thirty-seven demonstrations organized by black students in colleges and universities across the nation. The protesters, many of whom were on sports scholarships, demanded better treatment from white coaches, improved accommodation and better recreational facilities. In addition they campaigned for the hiring of more African American instructors and the introduction of Black Studies programmes.

In the early 1970s Muhammad Ali achieved vindication in the boxing ring as well as in the courts. Regaining his licence to fight in 1970, his first attempt to regain his world crown ended in failure, when he lost to Joe Frazier in 1971. The setback proved to be only temporary. On 30 October 1974 Ali again became World Heavyweight Champion, besting titleholder George Foreman. Fittingly, the contest, dubbed the 'Rumble in the Jungle', took place in the black African republic of Zaire. Two other victories in rematches against Frazier, in January 1974 and October 1975, confirmed that Ali, as he had always claimed, truly was 'The Greatest'.

The black student protests of 1968 typified a new mood of racial pride and militant assertiveness among young African Americans in the late 1960s. More than any other individual Malcolm X was the leading inspiration for radical black activists. In his years as a spokesman for the Nation of Islam he demonstrated considerable foresight in his appreciation of the power of the new medium of television. A regular contributor on news and political discussion programmes, he both alarmed whites and won admiration from black ghetto residents for his uncompromising views.

Breaking with the NOI in early 1964 he went on to become an influential independent commentator and thinker on racial issues in his own right. Malcolm's assassination, in February 1965, only served to enhance his standing in African American communities. This was reinforced by the publication of his book, *The Autobiography of Malcolm X*, the same year.

The story of his life as told to black journalist Alex Haley, *The*

Autobiography stressed the need for greater racial pride and consciousness. An inspiration for later Black Power radicals, the book demonstrated profound understanding of how white-dominated American culture reinforced racial prejudice and low black self-esteem. It highlighted how, in diverse ways, African Americans were encouraged to believe themselves to be inferior to whites.

The achievements of black artists, writers and leaders in history were routinely ignored in High School primers. In the English language concepts of whiteness were generally associated with things good and wholesome, whilst blackness most commonly had negative connotations. In fashion white concepts of beauty were advanced as the ideal. Black Americans were thus encouraged to buy skin-lightening cosmetics and use chemicals to straighten, or 'conk', their hair. The obvious implication was that their natural ethnic appearance was unattractive and something of which to be ashamed.

Profound in his understanding of the problems faced by black Americans, Malcolm X was unable to provide easy solutions for them. In the last months of his life he embarked on a process of reflection and spiritual enlightenment that was incomplete at the time of death. Although still influenced by Black Nationalism he appeared to soften his views on integration. In 1964 he converted to orthodox Islam and was moved by the feeling of multiracial brotherhood he experienced on a pilgrimage, or Hajj, to Mecca. At the same time he showed an interest in revolutionary socialism, and argued for the need to see the black liberation struggle in a global context. He believed that African Americans needed to identify more strongly with Third World black independence movements.

These competing, and often conflicting, aspirations became a source of weakness and division for later Black Power radicals. Some groups chose to focus on cultural nationalism. In 1965 the writer and poet LeRoi Jones opened the Black Arts Repertory Theater/School (BARTS) in Harlem. In 1966 he organized a Black Arts festival in Newark, New Jersey, and was a leading inspiration in the creation of a national Black Arts Movement that resulted in the opening of some 800 black theatres and cultural centres across the nation.

Moving to California in 1967, Jones adopted the new name of Amiri Baraka and joined the United Slaves organization founded in the state two years earlier by Maulenga Ron Karenga. A play on the initials of the United States, the name of the group also implied the need for racial unity, 'us' as opposed to 'them'. In common with other African Americans in the late 1960s, Karenga's followers adopted African hairstyles and clothes, wearing loose brightly coloured 'dashiki' shirts. Karenga laid down a distinctive black philosophy, the 'Seven Principles of Kawaida', drawn from African tribal culture and traditions. US converts were expected to live by these teachings and to observe Kwanzaa, a holiday purported to be of African origin.

Highly critical of Karenga, the Black Panthers, a radical organization founded in Oakland, California in 1966, came to view revolutionary socialism as the solution for the problems faced by black Americans. From this perspective Karenga's cultural nationalism was misguided and harmful. It encouraged black Americans to devote their energies to symbolic acts instead of focusing on the real issue of class struggle. Moreover, such 'pork chop' nationalism could also encourage reactionary and oppressive political ideologies, as was the case with the regime of 'Papa Doc' Duvalier in Haiti.

At odds with Karenga, the Panthers also had strong disagreements with other leading figures in the Black Power movement like Stokely Carmichael of SNCC and Roy Innis of CORE. By the late 1960s SNCC and CORE had become all-black organizations following the expulsion and voluntary exodus of white members. Carmichael advocated racially autonomous initiatives within the United States and international ties with black African countries. Panther leaders Huey Newton and Bobby Seale saw such ventures as wrongheaded. Instead, black activists should seek to ally themselves with other radical groups to form a multiracial class-based alliance.

The conflicting philosophies of groups like the United Slaves and the Panthers should not be exaggerated. In part their differences were simply a matter of emphasis. Spokesmen like Baraka and Karenga did not see reverence for African culture as an end in itself, but rather as first step to mobilize black American communities in support of political initiatives.

Similarly, the Panthers were not unaware of the positive role that culture could play in the freedom struggle. In an attempt to popularize their political message in the ghettos the Panthers even established their own record label, Seize The Time, and a Panther Soul group, The Lumpen, regaled listeners with songs like 'Old Pig Nixon' set to the tune of 'Old Man River'.

Such considerations notwithstanding, ideological disagreements between spokesmen like Karenga, Newton and Carmichael were a major source of disunity, to the point where violent clashes between United Slaves converts and Panther activists became common in black ghetto districts in California. The vague meaning of the slogan Black Power, and the diverse and conflicting groups and individuals that it attracted, was both a fundamental strength and weakness of the Black Power movement.

In the early 1970s cinema and television began to respond to the rise of Black Power. In the film industry the most notable development was the emergence of the 'Blaxploitation' genre. Typically low-cost productions targeted at black inner-city audiences, Blaxploitation films featured black actors in all the leading roles and introduced a new screen stereotype, the 'Superspade'. This black hero, almost always male, lived life on the edge. He coolly overcame physical danger on a daily basis, yet still found time for innumerable casual sexual relationships with beautiful women of all races. His business activities often placed him on the wrong side of the law but he lived by his own moral code and took pride in his ethnic background.

White characters usually appeared only briefly in Blaxploitation productions. If given more substantive roles they played racists who met their come-uppance at the hands of the black star. Women featured more prominently, but they were usually no more than passing sexual conquests for the male lead. The Blaxploitation genre, even more than the Black Power movement, was notable for its male chauvinism. There were occasional Blaxploitation heroines, such as Pam Grier in the title role of *Cleopatra Jones* (1973), but these characters did not provide role models with which most women could identify. Instead they were more the products of male fantasies, being slim, sensual and with insatiable sexual appetites.

The first major Blaxploitation productions were *Cotton Comes to Harlem* (1970) and *Sweet Sweetback's Baadasssss Song* (1971), costing $1.2 million and $500,000 to make respectively. Produced, written and directed by black filmmaker Melvin Van Peebles, the latter production was shot in just nineteen days. Grainy and basic in film quality, it went on to gross more than $10 million in its first year at the box office, compared to $5.5 million achieved by *Cotton Comes To Harlem*.

The success of the two films reflected the power of black audiences at the box office. In 1967 black Americans comprised 15 per cent of the US population but made up 30 per cent of film audiences in large cities where many cinemas were located.

Other filmmakers, mostly white, sought to emulate Van Peebles in taking advantage of this market, and a succession of Blaxploitation productions resulted. Some of these, like *Shaft* (1971), starring Richard Roundtree, had genuine artistic merit. Playing a black detective created by white novelist Ernest Tidyman, Rountree reprised his role in two later films, *Shaft's Big Score* (1972) and *Shaft in Africa* (1973).

Other Blaxploitation productions were less memorable and were often little more than crude attempts by white directors and producers to appeal to black audiences. This failing, combined with the blatant sexism of many Blaxploitation films, resulted in the genre being held in low esteem by many film critics and historians.

To some extent this perception is justified. At the same time Blaxploitation productions constituted a breakthrough. For the first time African Americans were cast in strong leading roles and were portrayed as more than capable of triumphing over white adversaries. The best productions were a genuine attempt to help bring about what Malcolm X had called the 'de-colonization of the black mind'. In the words of Van Peebles, they sought to 'reclaim the black spirit' from 'centuries of manipulation' by the white 'power structure'.

Television executives, targeting predominantly white audiences, generally made less effort to accommodate black tastes. *The Mod Squad* (1968–73), a comedy detective series, starred three undercover cops, 'one black, one white, one blonde'. The black lead, played by Clarence Williams III, sported a luxuriant Afro haircut in what was an obvious attempt to appeal to the Black Power generation.

The risk in creating characters with black-appeal was that they might alienate white advertising sponsors and viewers. *The Outcasts*, a western series starring Otis Young as a black bounty hunter in the post-Civil War era, highlighted the problem. Race proud, and bitter about the suffering of blacks under slavery, Young's character became a subject of controversy. The series ran for just one season on ABC in 1968–9.

Acknowledging the troubled nature of the times some series

sought to introduce greater social realism. *Room 222* (1969–74) focused on the experiences of a young black teacher, played by Lloyd Hines, working in an integrated Los Angeles High School.

A Norman Lear creation, *All in the Family* (1971–9), introduced the nation to the bigoted Archie Bunker played by Carroll O'Conner. Inspired by a British television character, Alf Garnett, Bunker regularly engaged in arguments with family, friends and neighbours, putting forward his prejudiced views on almost all issues. Compelling, in a repellent sort of way, Archie became a curiously endearing character for American audiences. His one redeeming quality was that his views were so absurd and ill informed as to suggest that they were prompted by ignorance rather than malice. At the same time the uncomfortable suspicion lingered that some white viewers found him appealing because they secretly empathized with his opinions.

Good Times, another Norman Lear creation, ran on CBS from 1974–9. Focusing on the daily life of a black family in the South Side of Chicago, the series initially combined humour with a sympathetic portrayal of real issues. This balance did not last. Looking for easy laughs, the show increasingly concentrated on the comic antics of the family's buffoon like son, 'JJ', played by Jimmie Walker. A racial caricature, JJ, bore an uncomfortable resemblance to minstrel stereotypes of an earlier era.

The changing nature of *Good Times* was part of a wider trend on American television in the 1970s. Television stations increasingly moved to a 'happy talk' format. Instead of providing serious commentary on contemporary issues programme makers provided viewers with escapist, light entertainment and comedy programmes.

The Flip Wilson Show (1970–4) on NBC became one of the most popular programmes on television, attracting at its peak audiences of more than 40 million. In humorous sketches, the show's African American host entertained viewers by adopting a succession of comic black characters like 'Reverend Leroy', 'Sonny the Janitor' and 'Charley the Chef'. Bearing little resemblance to the realities of inner-city life, Wilson's creations complied with stereotyped images of African Americans held by successive generations of white audiences.

At the same time that they adopted a 'happy talk' format national TV networks also began to downplay coverage of depressing news stories, like ghetto riots and incidents involving racial conflict. Ever responsive to the changing tastes of their viewers, television programme makers sensed a new mood among audiences. After almost two decades of domestic conflict many Americans were beginning to experience compassion fatigue when faced with intractable problems like black civil rights and inner-city poverty.

CHAPTER FIVE

African Americans in US society since 1976

After the turbulent years of the late 1960s and early 1970s it was predictable that a period of conservative reaction would follow. In the last quarter of the twentieth century the high hopes of the Black Power era increasingly gave way to disillusionment.

Under the Presidency of Democrat Jimmy Carter, 1977–81, economic recession led to rising poverty and deteriorating living conditions in the inner cities. During the 1980s and early 1990s the economic policies of the conservative Republican administrations of Ronald Reagan, 1981–9, and George Bush, 1989–93, exacerbated the situation. Showing more concern for the greedy than the needy, Reagan cut taxes and reduced expenditure on welfare programmes.

The administrations of William 'Bill' Clinton, 1993–2001, saw no major improvement. More compassionate in outlook than his two predecessors, Clinton's planned reforms, most notably in health care, were blocked by Republican majorities in Congress. Reflecting the conservative nature of US public opinion, Clinton also projected the image of a 'New Democrat', committing his party to greater restraint in government expenditure and tougher policies on crime and welfare provision.

In November 2000 the election of Republican George W. Bush to the White House ensured the continuation of conservative policies. The son of a former President, George W. Bush shared the right-wing ideological convictions of his father as well as the family name.

African Americans, disproportionately subject to economic and social deprivation, were hard hit by all of these developments. Although increasing numbers of black Americans in the 1980s and 1990s enjoyed a middle-class lifestyle many were not so fortunate.

In the 1990s a third of African American families lived in poverty compared to only 10 per cent of white households.

In inner-city ghettos rising levels of drug dependency and violent crime added to the problems created by deteriorating social infrastructures. In 1990 610,000 black American men in their twenties – a quarter of all African American males in this age group – were in jail or on probation. In comparison just 436,000 African American males aged 20–29 were in higher education.

Declining living standards were accompanied by worsening race relations. Under the Reagan and Bush administrations African Americans were increasingly depicted as welfare spongers or violent criminals. Across the nation reports of serious incidents between police forces and African Americans became common. Often attracting high profile media coverage, such news stories highlighted the racist attitudes of police officers and deepened longstanding distrust of law enforcement agencies within black communities.

In another disturbing development there was a significant rise in the number of white supremacist groups and extreme right-wing militias. Pseudo-religious organizations like Christian Identity advanced a theology that portrayed Jews as the spawn of Satan and African Americans as subhuman 'mud people'. Aryan Nations urged followers to prepare for a racial holy war. *The Turner Diaries* (1978), a racist fantasy novel, became cult reading among supporters of the far right. Set in the near future, the book portrayed a successful paramilitary coup by white supremacists.

Limited in scale, race-hate organizations were able to gain considerable publicity for their views. Taking advantage of new technology racial extremists launched some 250 Internet websites to disseminate their ideas by the end of the 1990s. A small number of activists, most infamously Timothy McVeigh, resorted to acts of terrorism or racial violence in an attempt to advance their cause. In 2001 McVeigh was executed by federal authorities for his involvement in the 1995 Oklahoma City bombing, in which 168 people had been killed and more than 500 injured.

Affirmative action programmes, established in the 1960s and early 1970s to advance ethnic minority groups in employment and education, continued to operate in the 1980s and 1990s. Vigorously defended by black political leaders and civil rights activists, such initiatives nonetheless became subject to increasing criticism. Conservative commentators criticized positive discrimination programmes as unfairly favouring African Americans at the expense of whites.

Such arguments typified a reaction against what was perceived as an excessive concern for political correctness in earlier decades. In this vein black collectibles, unfashionable between the 1950s and early 1970s, again became popular. In the 1980s a Black Memorabilia Collectors Association was founded, and by 1994 some 45,000 Americans, including 9,000 African Americans, were active enthusiasts of the genre.

There were a variety of reasons for this interest. Some collectors claimed to value black memorabilia for their craftsmanship and artistic merit that outweighed any offensive racial imagery. Black aficionados argued that such collectibles were artefacts that needed to be preserved as reminders of how blacks had been perceived by previous generations of white Americans. For middle-class black enthusiasts the memorabilia served as a reminder of their own success in overcoming the disadvantages experienced by their ancestors. Collecting such objects demonstrated that they were self-confident and at ease with this new found professional status.

The motives of other collectors were less complex and more suspect. Many enthusiasts purchased cheap reproductions of black memorabilia, rather than the more expensive originals, suggesting that there were other reasons for the revival of the genre than just an admiration for antique craftsmanship. In the Reagan and Bush era it became increasingly fashionable not to support civil rights causes. Taking a stand against political correctness became more acceptable, even commendable, in that it demonstrated the capacity for individual thought in questioning dogma. The purchase of black memorabilia, in part, represented a conscious act of defiance against such values.

Developments in the radio industry during the 1980s and the 1990s reflected the wider changes taking place in US society. In urban areas newly affluent African American professionals followed the example of their white counterparts in moving out of the inner cities into the suburbs. Faced with declining audiences black-appeal stations responded in different ways to maintain ratings.

One strategy was 'format segmentation', targeting broadcasting at specific age and income groups, for example programmes on Hip Hop culture for young urban adults. Other broadcasters sought to broaden their audiences, in particular seeking to attract more white listeners by developing greater 'crossover' appeal. Typical of this approach was the emergence of the 'urban contemporary' format which involved playing music by white artists, like Elton John, in addition to recordings by black performers. If successful as a ratings ploy, this meant that by the late 1970s many black-appeal stations were beginning to lose their distinctive ethnic character. The airtime devoted to music by black performers was also reduced, as stations targeted at white audiences did not respond in kind by playing more records by African American artists.

More encouraging was the creation of the American Urban Radio Networks (AURN) in 1991 brought about by the merger of the Sheridan Broadcasting Corporation (SBC) and the National Black Network (NBN). The new organization, owned by African American Ron Davenport, was easily the nation's largest black-run radio network and the third biggest network in the entire industry. In the 1990s AURN, with its headquarters in Pittsburgh, built up a clientele of more than 250 station affiliates and its programmes were accessible to over 90 per cent of black Americans.

Such African American success was rare. The free market philosophy of the 1980s and 1990s resulted in a gradual deregulation of radio broadcasting by the federal government. This culminated in the 1996 Telecommunications Act which made it possible for one company to own up to eight radio stations (five FM and three AM) in any single market and set no national limit on the number of stations that could be controlled by a single owner.

The major beneficiaries of this change were business conglomerates that embarked on aggressive takeovers and buyouts of smaller competitors. By the end of the decade two broadcasting giants had emerged, Westinghouse/CBS with 175 stations and $1,500,000,000 in annual revenues, and Hicks, Muse, Tate and Furst Holdings, with 395 stations and $1,460,000,000 in yearly income.

Small black-run stations were unable to compete with such large enterprises when it came to attracting advertising revenue. The development of expensive new digital technology, that only large well-resourced companies could afford, further undermined their position. The largest African American chain of radio stations, Radio One owned by Cathy Hughes, comprised just nine outlets in and around Washington DC. For the first time in decades the number of black-owned commercial radio stations actually declined in the 1990s.

To some extent this was offset by a growth in the number of public service or non-commercial black stations, mostly run by community groups and colleges like Howard University in Washington, DC. Even in this field the advances were modest. In the mid-1990s just 2.5 per cent of all public radio outlets were black-run. Moreover, federal funding cutbacks during the 1980s and 1990s made it difficult for public service stations to remain viable.

In sport black competitors made some major advances during the last decades of the twentieth century. At the 1984 Olympic Games in Los Angeles forty of the forty-nine medals won by the United States in track and field events were gained by black athletes. In boxing African Americans were responsible for ten of the eleven medals won by US fighters. By 1998 African Americans comprised 80 per cent of the players in the NBA national basketball league, 60 per cent of players in the National Football League (NFL), and 25 per cent of players in Major League baseball.

The best African American competitors, like basketball legend Michael Jordan, enjoyed lucrative sponsorship deals with leading white-owned companies, such as fast food chains, like MacDonald's, and sportswear manufacturers Nike.

Albeit a breakthrough, success came at a price. One consequence of black sporting success was that it encouraged African American children to elevate sporting prowess above academic achievement. Ironically, this echoed the industrial education movement in the closing years of the nineteenth century, when educators advocated training in manual skills for African American and white working-class children rather than the study of more intellectual subjects.

In the 1980s and 1990s the preoccupation of black children with success on the sports field was in some respects even more disturbing. Inevitably, only a tiny proportion of teenage athletes would ever be able to pursue a professional career in their chosen sport, leaving the large majority disillusioned and ill-equipped to seek alternative employment.

Responding to this concern, in 1986 the National Collegiate Athletics Association (NCAA) introduced Proposition 48 raising the academic standards required of students applying for sports scholarships in colleges and universities. The initiative divided the African American community. Some commentators supported the measure but others condemned it as racially discriminatory, leading to a disproportionate number of black students being rejected for college places because of their failure to meet the new standards.

Almost all of the new black sporting superstars carefully avoided speaking out on controversial racial issues. Multiracial golfing sensation Tiger Woods objected to the fact that he was described as African American at all. Instead he preferred to categorize himself as 'Cablinasian', because he was part Caucasian, part black, part native American and part Asian.

The reticence of black sporting celebrities to identify themselves with civil rights issues reflected the fact that their wealth distanced them from the concerns of ordinary African Americans. Commercial interest was also a factor. In the conservative climate of the 1980s and 1990s an outspoken stance on sensitive political topics risked the loss of revenue from multi-million dollar advertising deals.

If African American sportsmen were well paid by sponsors, the images of black sports celebrities in advertising continued to be stereotyped. White athletes were typically depicted in adverts as having reached the peak of their profession by dint of hard work, quick intelligence and strength of character. In contrast, their black counterparts were depicted as being successful because of their natural physical strength and talent. They were also more likely to be portrayed in a violent or sexually suggestive manner.

Sports commentators also persisted in stereotyped racial thinking. In the 1990s reporters still compared black sportsmen to monkeys and commented on their 'natural' athletic ability, whereas 'thinking' white competitors were praised for strategic mastery. In January 1988 Jimmy 'the Greek' Snyder sparked a nationwide controversy when he suggested that black athletics had an innate advantage over their white counterparts because their slave ancestors had been selectively bred to enhance their physical strength.

Perpetuating hackneyed racist attitudes about the susceptibility of African Americans to gluttony, a number of black stars were given nicknames in the sports press that emphasized their ability to consume almost limitless amounts of food. In the NFL the Chicago Bears were thus aided by the talents of William 'the Refrigerator' Perry, whilst the Dallas Cowboys were able to call on the resources of Nate 'the Kitchen' Newton.

The perception of black athletes as sexual predators, and prone to violence, became overt in high-profile cases where black sporting celebrities breached accepted social norms or engaged in unacceptable personal conduct. Once portrayed as a positive role model by the media, former NFL star O. J. Simpson became demonized in 1995 as a result of his trial for the murder of his white wife Nicole and one of her close friends. Although acquitted, the majority of white Americans remained convinced of Simpson's guilt, believing that defence lawyers had enabled him to escape justice by portraying him as a victim of police racism.

This unease was reinforced by a 1997 civil lawsuit brought against Simpson by families of the murder victims. The lower burden of proof demanded by the civil courts made it easier for the prosecution to argue the case and Simpson was ordered to pay $35.5 million in damages. Although free from imprisonment, his financial resources were seriously depleted and he became a social outcast.

In boxing African American Mike Tyson experienced a similar fall from grace. In 1987 he became undisputed World Heavyweight Champion at just twenty-one years of age and was already hailed as one of the all-time greats of the sport. By the 1990s Tyson's unacceptable personal behaviour resulted in his public shaming and humiliation. In 1992 he was jailed for the rape of a black beauty contestant, Desiree Washington. Released in 1995, in 1999 he was again imprisoned for a road rage assault.

Tyson's legal troubles were accompanied by declining performances in the ring. In 1990 Tyson unexpectedly lost his world title to James 'Buster' Douglass. Briefly regaining the crown in 1996, he was again defeated the same year by Evander Holyfield. In a 1997 rematch with Holyfield Tyson was disqualified for biting off part of his opponent's ear and banned from the sport altogether. Eventually regaining his license to fight, Tyson's career appeared to be finally over when he was defeated by the new titleholder, Lennox Lewis, in June 2002.

The downfall of both Simpson and Tyson can be attributed to their own personal failings. At the same time they symbolized the nation's troubled race relations. Condemned by the majority of white Americans, the two men retained strong support among African Americans, many of whom perceived them as victims of the white-run media and legal system.

The strong support given to Tyson and Simpson by leading black spokespersons, such as Louis Farrakhan of the Nation of Islam, highlighted continuing sexist attitudes within the African American community. Despite evidence that both men were guilty of physical and sexual abuse against women, male black commentators often appeared indifferent to the suffering of the female victims.

Stereotyped racial attitudes exerted a powerful influence in the sporting arena. Positions on the playing field that were perceived as requiring intelligence or leadership qualities continued to be dominated by whites, even in sports where the majority of players were black. In baseball black players were largely confined to outfield positions whereas whites were more often deployed as pitchers or catchers. Similarly, whites were more likely to play as centres or quarterbacks in the NFL. One result of this thinking was the practice of 'stacking', requiring black players to compete for a limited number of positions, and thereby restricting their opportunities to break through into the first team.

Off the field of play whites filled the majority of coaching positions. In 1998 African Americans comprised just 2 per cent of coaches in Major League baseball and 7 per cent in the NFL, yet black Americans made up around 12.5 per cent of the total US population. Basketball, where 14 per cent of coaches were black, did reflect the racial balance of the nation but given that almost all leading players in the sport were African American this statistic was unimpressive.

Whites occupied almost all business and managerial roles in sport. This, combined with their predominance in coaching, led some academic commentators, like John Hoberman, to conclude that, in the early years of the twenty-first century, a 'colonial arrangement' prevailed in American sport. 'Sweating' and 'half-dressed' black athletes were instructed and disciplined by 'well dressed and well groomed' white handlers. Even if highly paid for their endeavours, the position of African American sportsmen can also be seen as reminiscent of the role filled by their slave ancestors.

In the music industry the national weariness with political radicalism in the late 1970s was reflected in the rise of Disco, a music and dance trend that had its origins in black and gay nightclubs. Glitzy and narcissistic, the new craze was devoid of political meaning. Instead young Americans of all races sought escape from the economic hardships of the Carter years by dancing away the weekends.

Despite its African American roots the new culture only achieved mass popularity after it was portrayed on film in *Saturday Night Fever* (1977) by white actor John Travolta, and with music and lyrics by white super-group, the Bee Gees. By the end of the decade Disco had gone out of fashion, much to the relief of older Americans who, as always, neither liked nor understood the music enjoyed by their children. Parental disapproval was in part simply a result of the generation gap, but it also had racial connotations, reflecting the concern of conservative white opinion at the perceived 'unhealthy' influence of African American culture on the nation's youth.

The major development of the early 1980s was the emergence of Hip Hop, a black inner-city youth culture. Reflecting the alienation and social and economic deprivation of ghetto communities Hip Hop expression took a variety of forms, including break-dancing, graffiti art and a new style in clothing that was typified by the wearing of baseball caps or woollen hats, over-large jackets and trousers, and heavy duty boots or trainers.

Rap music became the most important embodiment of the new culture. First restricted to urban black communities, by the early 1980s Rap began to reach wider audiences. In 1984 *Run DMC*, by the group Run DMC, became the first Rap album to achieve major crossover success. In the years 1987–90 Public Enemy became the first Rap superstar group. In marked contrast to the escapism of Disco, Rap lyrics articulated the realities of inner-city life and videos accompanying the music were shot in real ghetto locations.

During the 1980s the geographical centre of Rap was the east coast, most particularly New York City. By the early 1990s this situation changed with the emergence of a succession of major West Coast artists. An early indication of this development was the release of the 1988 album *Straight Outta Compton* by Los Angeles group Niggaz Wit Attitude (NWA). An instant success, the album quickly sold more than 2 million copies and marked the rise of a new genre within the music, Gangsta Rap, or G-Funk, as it was also known.

Highly controversial, Gangsta Rappers incorporated images of guns and violence into their lyrics as a mode of artistic self-expression. Their music was rooted in the LA street gang culture of the Crips and the Bloods and reflected the distrust of any form of authority, most especially white-dominated law enforcement

95

agencies, that prevailed within black inner-city communities. In this vein *Straight Outta Compton* compared life in the ghetto to the Vietnam War and included a song with the title 'Fuck the Police'.

A number of Gangsta lyrics engaged in revenge fantasies with white law enforcement officers being gunned down by black ghetto protagonists. In 1992 the song 'Cop Killer', on the *Body Count* album released by Ice-T, provoked outrage in the media. President George Bush denounced the record as 'sick' and the Combined Law Enforcement Associations of Texas (CLEAT) called for a public boycott of Time Warner, the company that owned Ice-T's record label. The song was cut from later editions of the album.

Violence against women was a common and disturbing theme in Gangsta recordings, amounting to what historian Michael Dyson has described as 'femiphobia'. Lyrics routinely referred to women as bitches and whores and depicted them as objects for male sexual gratification rather than as equal partners. The most extreme manifestation of this tendency came in the sub-genre of 'Booty Rap' in which lyrics focused almost exclusively on violent and graphic sexual imaginings.

In 1990 the release 'As Nasty As They Wanna Be' by the group 2 Live Crew created especial controversy. Made up of explicit numbers that described almost every imaginable form of sexual activity, the album became the first music recording to be declared legally obscene in a federal district court. Some female Rap groups like the New York based Bytches with Problems (BWP), and Hoez Wit Attitude (HWA) from LA, could be equally graphic in lyrics about sex, but most Rap artists were male. This reinforced the impression that the music exulted in the denigration of women as a means of boosting male self-esteem.

Loyalty to a gang or 'crew' was a recurring feature in Gangsta Rap. This was apparent in the image of the 'dogg' that was most notably popularized by Snoop Doggy Dogg in his controversial 1993 debut solo album *Doggystyle*. Evoking the image of a downtrodden animal, the dog, or 'dogg', surmounted the hardships of daily life, prowling the neighbourhood, or 'hood', in packs. Unfortunately, such identification with canine virtue further encouraged derogatory references to women as 'bitches'. The cover of the *Doggystyle* CD featured a cartoon representation of a randy male dog with a long tail, and in suggestive lyrics on the album Snoop boasted about 'burying his bone'.

Preoccupation with violent early death was another strong theme in Gangsta recordings. Artists frequently fantasized about their own death, either in violent shootouts or in executions sanctioned by the state. After leaving NWA Ice Cube's 1990 debut solo album, *Amerikkka's Most Wanted*, opened with lyrics describing his being marched to the electric chair. Founded in 1992, by fellow NWA member Dr Dre and Marion 'Suge' Knight, the leading Rap label of the mid-1990s was Death Row Records.

In a 1996 video recording of his song 'I Ain't Mad at Cha', leading Death Row artist Tupac Shakur acted out his being gunned to death by an imaginary assailant. In the 1992 film *Juice* the character played by Shakur also met a violent death. Similarly in a 2002 Hollywood production, *Monster's Ball*, east-coast Rapper Sean 'Puff Daddy' Combs played a death row prisoner.

In another central image, the autopsy was frequently used in Gangsta numbers to initiate discussion of the dead body, the marks of violent death and reflection on lost life. Using this device to highlight his rejection of traditional American values, Ice Cube had the cover of his second solo album, *Death Certificate* (1991), depict himself standing in mock mourning over a corpse laid out on a slab that was identified by a toe tag as 'Uncle Sam'.

Often the violent incidents described by Gangsta Rappers in their lyrics seemed to reflect the realities of their daily lives. The seeming contempt for women of Rap stars appeared to be confirmed when in 1991 Dr Dre assaulted music show host Dee Barnes, and in 1994 Tupac Shakur was jailed for the sexual assault of a female fan in a hotel room.

Shakur was not the only Rap artist to face imprisonment. In 1994 Dr Dre was jailed for six months for probation violations following earlier convictions for violent assault and drunk driving. In 1996 his Death Row cofounder Suge Knight, who had an even more violent track record, was jailed for nine years. Tried for murder the same year, Snoop Doggy Dogg was more fortunate, receiving a not guilty verdict. In March 2002 Sean Combs was similarly acquitted of gun possession charges relating to a 1999 shooting that had threatened to send him to jail for up to fifteen years. Six months later, in September 2002, Combs was ordered by a North Carolina court to pay $2.45 million in damages to the victim of an alleged assault by bodyguards hired by the Rap star.

97

In two tragic cases of the 1990s Rap artists were the victims of violence rather than the perpetrators. On 7 September 1996 Tupac Shakur was shot dead by an unknown assailant after surviving an earlier shooting in 1994. No one was arrested for the killing. In spring the following year Shakur's rival, Biggie Smalls, who was suspected by some of being implicated in the murder, was also shot to death in a possible revenge killing.

Evoking painful memories of these incidents on 30 October 2002 Jam Master Jay of Run DMC was shot dead by an unknown assailant in a New York city recording studio. In contrast to Tupac Shakur and Biggie Smalls Jay had distanced himself from the Gangsta genre and projected an image of mainstream respectability.

Unsurprisingly, the Gangsta Rap phenomenon attracted criticism from a variety of groups and individuals. Women and conservative moralists took exception to the music for obvious reasons. More liberal commentators criticized the lack of political content in Rap, and black leaders condemned it for perpetuating negative images of African American communities.

Supporters of the genre responded to these allegations in a number of ways. They argued that the themes in Gangsta lyrics simply reflected the realities of ghetto life. Songs like 'Cop Killer' did not incite violence against the police, they merely articulated commonly held views within the ghetto. Significantly, the National Black Police Association condemned the campaign against 'Cop Killer', arguing that the real issue of concern was the numerous authenticated reports of police violence against black ghetto residents that had inspired the song's sentiments.

Rap artists like Ice-T were quick to draw distinctions between the fantasy lyrics of their songs and real life. There was little evidence to suggest that Rap lyrics were directly responsible for any acts of ghetto violence. In the tradition of 'signifying' within the African American community it was common for singers to boast of their sexual conquests or bad character, but black audiences understood that these claims were purely imaginary.

To some extent the denunciations of Rap can be seen as part of a recurring cycle in American popular culture. For almost a century parents and grandparents condemned youth culture as heralding the end of civilization, overlooking the fact that their own musical tastes had often been denounced in equally strong terms by earlier generations.

At the same time some criticisms of Rap were hard to dismiss. Although some recordings did try to project constructive themes, 'message rap', most Rap lyrics were nihilistic in tone. References towards women in the music did appear to be gratuitously offensive. In a perceptive observation feminist writer bell hooks argued that Rappers acted out stereotyped images of black American males as violent and sexually predatory to pander to voyeuristic white consumers, who comprised 70 per cent of the purchasers of Rap records. If correct this meant that Rap artists, rather than being fearless social rebels, were more akin to black minstrel performers of the late nineteenth century who demeaned themselves for financial rewards.

By the late 1990s the Gangsta Rap phenomenon had lost impetus. Artists had run out of themes to explore and their lyrics no longer had the same power to shock. Several leading figures in the genre were either dead or in jail and Death Row Records folded in 1997 following the imprisonment of Suge Knight. Other Rappers seemed to mellow with age. Dr Dre married and had children, as did Snoop Doggy Dogg. In March 2002 Sean Combs thanked God for his courtroom acquittal and adopted the less challenging alias of P. Diddy.

At the start of the new millennium the most significant development was the emergence of white Rap superstar Marshall Mathers, better known as Eminem. Although there had been successful white Rap acts before, like Vanilla Ice in the early 1990s, they had not lasted. They lacked street credibility in a genre that was so deeply rooted in black ghetto culture. This was not true of Eminem who had a troubled childhood, much of which was spent in a disadvantaged and predominantly black neighbourhood in Detroit.

Promoted by Dr Dre, Eminem's first two albums, *The Slim Shady LP* (1999) and *The Marshall Mathers LP* (2000), were an enormous commercial success. The themes in Eminem's lyrics were similar to those of earlier black Rappers, but coming from a white artist they appeared fresh and shocking, making him a cult figure for teenage audiences worldwide.

In May 2002 he released a third successful album, *The Eminem Show*. At the MTV Music Awards in August 2002 Eminem's video *Without Me* was voted Best Male Video, Best Rap Video and overall Best Video of the Year, suggesting that he would continue to be a dominant force in Rap for the foreseeable future.

Hollywood responded in a variety of ways to the changes in US race relations in the last decades of the twentieth century. Some productions examined racial issues in a historical context, such as *Glory* (1989), the story of a black regiment, the 54th Massachusetts Volunteers, during the Civil War, and the courtroom drama *Amistad* (1997).

Driving Miss Daisy (1989), with Jessica Tandy and Morgan Freeman, was an unexpected box office success. The film viewed race relations in Georgia during the 1950s and 1960s through the eyes of a retired Jewish schoolteacher, Miss Daisy, and her black chauffeur, Hoke. More controversially, *Mississippi Burning* (1988) was based on the murder of civil rights workers, James Chaney, Andrew Goodman and Michael Schwerner in Mississippi in 1964. The film was criticized for distorting the facts of the case and for containing no major black characters, despite its civil rights theme. Instead the heroes of the storyline were two white FBI agents played by Willem Dafoe and Gene Hackman.

Albeit flawed, *Mississippi Burning* was one of comparatively few films to examine the civil rights struggles of the 1950s and 1960s. In marked contrast, a succession of films focused on the Vietnam War, the other major issue that had divided Americans in the 1960s. One obvious reason for this was that the anguish caused by the war was largely an issue of the past, in contrast to the nation's unresolved racial problems.

Filmmakers were less reluctant to explore racial issues with an overseas setting. A number of productions in the late 1980s centred on the anti-apartheid struggle in South Africa, such as *Cry Freedom* (1987), *A World Apart* (1988) and *A Dry White Season* (1989). Albeit powerful condemnations of the country's minority white regime, a common weakness of these films was that they focused more on the hardships endured by liberal white activists against the system than the suffering of the majority black population.

This shortcoming was also true of other cinematic productions. *Out of Africa* (1985) starred Meryl Streep as a settler in Kenya with Robert Redford, playing a dashing aviator, providing her romantic interest. Native black Africans appeared only as servants and camp followers, the same roles that that been assigned to them in the Tarzan films of Johnny Weissmuller some fifty years earlier.

Similarly, in *Gorillas in the Mist* (1988), Sigourney Weaver starred as a lone heroine struggling to conserve the endangered mountain gorilla. Black characters in the storyline appeared either as subordinates awaiting her commands, or worse as greedy, brutish natives who ultimately murdered both the gorillas and Weaver for monetary gain. The film made no attempt to examine tribal culture or the system of economic exploitation that encouraged the killing of primates.

By the mid-1970s the continued domination of the world heavyweight boxing championship by African American fighters suggested that there was little prospect of a white contender emerging to reclaim the crown. Instead, the dream of a new great white hope was kept alive on the screen by Sylvester Stallone in *Rocky* (1976), and the unimaginatively titled sequels *Rocky II* (1979), *Rocky III* (1982), and *Rocky IV* (1985). The characterization of the films was also less than original. Playing a poor, inarticulate, Italian American Stallone captured the world title from defending black champion Apollo Creed, played by Carl Weathers. He then defended his crown against 'black brute', Clubber Lang, portrayed by B. A. Barracus.

In later storylines, rather than being adversaries, Stallone and Weathers had become close friends. This bonding between two male characters, one white, one black, was typical of numerous productions of the 1980s and 1990s. In the 1980s films of this type included *An Officer and a Gentleman* (1982), with Louis Gossett and Richard Gere, *Trading Places* (1983), with Dan Ackroyd and Eddie Murphy, and *Lethal Weapon* (1987), with Danny Glover and Mel Gibson. During the 1990s the pattern was continued with the likes of *Robin Hood, Prince of Thieves* (1991), with Kevin Costner and Morgan Freeman, *The Shawshank Redemption* (1994), with Morgan Freeman and Tim Robbins, and *Seven* (1995), with Morgan Freeman and Brad Pitt.

Dubbed 'buddy buddy' films by historian Donald Bogle, screen depictions of such relationships provided uplifting examples of interracial brotherhood. Ignoring the broader political, social and economic framework of race relations, such films suggested that race was an issue that could simply be resolved by well-intentioned individuals. The black character in the relationship was typically cut off from his ethnic roots, thus avoiding the need to consider the systematic economic and social deprivation suffered by African American communities.

There were other recurring features in 'buddy buddy' films. Whereas the white lead was often given a romantic interest the

African American co-star was typically celibate. Moreover, the friendship was often unequal in basis. In reprisals of the Huck Finn complex the black character frequently aided his white colleague through a period of personal crisis. This sometimes involved the black co-star acting as a mentor to his white friend, but there was little doubt as to which buddy would ultimately be the dominant character.

A significant development in the 1980s and 1990s was the emergence of a growing number of black directors, such as Euzhan Palcy, Mario Van Peebles and Spike Lee. In a series of usually low-budget productions these filmmakers examined a variety of controversial racial issues. In *Panther* (1995), Van Peebles traced the origins of the Black Panthers. In *Do The Right Thing* (1989), Spike Lee analysed the causes of a race riot and in *Jungle Fever* (1991) he explored the tensions caused by an interracial sexual relationship and ghetto drugs problems. In *Clockers* (1995) he examined this latter theme in more detail, highlighting the devastating impact of crack cocaine on inner-city communities. *Malcolm X* (1992), Lee's most ambitious production of the decade, told the life story of the martyred black icon. Unable to attract funding from white Hollywood backers, Lee was only able to complete this epic as a result of donations from black celebrities like Bill Cosby.

A new phenomenon of the 1990s was the Gangsta film, portraying the violent lives of young black Americans in the inner cities. Films in this category included John Singleton's *Boyz in the Hood* (1991), Mario Van Peebles's *New Jack City* (1991), *Menace II Society* (1993), by the Hughes brothers, Allen and Albert, and *Juice*, directed by Ernest R. Dickerson. Containing frequent references to Hip Hop culture such productions often starred real life Rap artists such as Ice T and Tupac Shakur.

Despite these developments, mainstream Hollywood productions of the 1980s and 1990s remained conservative in outlook. There still appeared to be racially sensitive areas that were off limits to directors. There was a reluctance to portray interracial sexual relationships, especially if they involved a white actress. This was despite the increasingly graphic depictions of trysts between white stars in productions like *Fatal Attraction* (1987) and *Basic Instinct* (1992). *Love Field* (1992), an interracial love drama set in the Kennedy era, with Michelle Pfeiffer and Dennis Haybert, was a creditable exception, but the film did poorly at the box office.

In an era when the success or failure of a film could depend on the audience appeal of its principal star, filmmakers seemed unwilling to give leading roles to black actors unless they appeared with a white co-star. The notable exception to this was in comedy. In a number of productions like *Beverley Hills Cop* (1984) and *Beverley Hills Cop II* (1987), black superstar Eddie Murphy was marketed as the main attraction to entice cinema audiences. In some films, like *The Nutty Professor* (1996) and *Dr Doolittle* (1998), the ethnic identity of the original white characters was even altered to allow for Murphy's appearance in the role.

At the same time, the roles played by Murphy attracted criticism from some commentators. In uncomfortable reminders of earlier minstrel traditions he often played exaggeratedly streetwise characters. Possessing a taste for extravagant living, these individuals attained their objectives by quick wit and fast-talking rather than through intellectual ability or hard work.

In *Coming To America* (1988), Murphy, cast as an African prince visiting New York, entertained audiences with comic stereotyped portrayals of tribal culture. Although Paul Hogan similarly lampooned his native Australia in several film incarnations as outback hero Mike 'Crocodile' Dundee, the context of the two roles was different. The historical experience of white Australians was not that of African Americans. They had not been subject to centuries of racial discrimination, enslavement and segregation.

By the 1980s and 1990s Sidney Poitier was no longer the only black Hollywood superstar. In addition to Eddie Murphy a number of black actors, like Denzel Washington and Morgan Freeman, became internationally acclaimed screen celebrities. Unfortunately this was less a case of 'we have overcome' than 'he has overcome', for the number of roles open to black women remained limited. In the 1980s and 1990s, although there were occasional film appearances by black musical celebrities, like Whitney Houston, Grace Jones and Diana Ross, Whoopi Goldberg was the only black actress to appear regularly in leading roles.

In the early years of the twenty-first century there were some indications that this situation might be about to change. At the annual Academy Awards Ceremony in April 2002 Halle Berry made screen history by becoming the first African American woman to win an Oscar as best actress in a leading role. Moreover, the film for which she was nominated, *Monster's Ball*, had strong racial

themes and featured Berry in an explicit interracial sexual relationship. In a night of unprecedented African American success
Denzel Washington was given an Oscar for best actor and Sidney
Poitier received a lifetime achievement award. It remained to be
seen however, whether the occasion was a one-off triumph or a
genuine departure from Hollywood's longstanding racial conservatism.

Developments in television during the last quarter of the twentieth
century were similar to those experienced in the film industry. A suc-
cession of historical dramas explored the nation's troubled racial past.
The earliest and most important of these, *Roots*, premiered in 1977.
Based on the best-selling book of the same name by journalist Alex
Haley, the mini-series ran for twelve hours and cost $6 million.
Portraying the experiences of Haley's slave ancestors it was an
enormous success. The final instalment, broadcast on 30 January,
was watched by almost 90 million viewers and over 140 million
Americans watched one or more episodes of the series.

A landmark in television history, *Roots* graphically depicted the
suffering of black Americans under slavery. History teachers across
the nation used extracts from the series as learning materials. At the
same time, *Roots* was less radical than it seemed. The focus of the
series on Haley's ancestors made it an odyssey of one family's
struggle rather than an indictment of the systematic economic
exploitation and racism that underpinned the institution of slavery.

The white characters in the story, afforded much larger roles
than in Haley's original book, were generally so unpleasant and
unsympathetic that few white viewers were likely to have identified
with them, or felt guilt over their actions. This also gave the
impression that a collection of depraved individuals, rather than the
nation as a whole, was responsible for slavery. This feeling was
reinforced by the fact that, despite their ordeal, when finally freed
the principal slave characters had faith in the American Dream of
material prosperity achieved through hard work.

The success of *Roots* led to a number of sequels. In February
1979 *Roots: The Next Generations* portrayed the experiences of
four generations of the Haley family since the abolition of slavery.
Running for fourteen hours and costing $16 million, the series was
almost as popular as the original, some 110 million Americans
watching one or more episodes. *Roots: The Gift* (1988) centred on
an improbable incident involving Haley's original slave ancestor

Kunte Kinte. In 1993 the mini-series *Queen* dramatized another Haley book, looking at the slave lives of his mother's side of the family. In 1998 *Mama Flora's Family* traced the early twentieth-century experiences of yet another Haley ancestor.

Other programme makers sought to emulate the *Roots* formula. *King* (1978), a six-hour mini-series starring Paul Winfield and Cicely Tyson, told the life story of Martin Luther King. *Freedom Road* (1979), based on the novel of the same name by Howard Fast, starred Muhammad Ali as a former slave who went on to became a US Senator. *Backstairs at the White House* (1979) focused on more humble lives. The nine-hour series drew inspiration from the real life experiences of two black domestic servants at the White House from the early twentieth century through to the 1950s.

By the mid-1980s costume dramas began to reflect the national mood of racial conservatism. *North and South* (1985) and *North and South: Book II* (1986), two twelve-hour mini-series set in the Civil War South, centred on the romantic, swashbuckling adventures of stereotyped white characters. These included Patrick Swayze as a gallant soldier and Lesley Anne Down as the mandatory southern belle. Although Kirstie Alley featured as a radical abolitionist, Virgilia, her character was portrayed as mentally unstable and met a tragic end together with her ex-slave husband.

Scarlett (1994), an eight-hour mini-series, was launched as a sequel to the Hollywood epic *Gone With the Wind*. Despite the many television incarnations of the Haley family the romanticized moonlight and magnolias image of the old South remained.

Period dramas that dealt overtly with racial issues had mixed fortunes. *Homefront* (1991–3) examined racial and class tensions in a small Ohio town just after the Second World War, and another series, *I'll Fly Away* (1991–3), was located in rural Georgia during the civil rights era of the 1950s and 1960s. Neither enjoyed popular appeal. In contrast *In the Heat of the Night*, a spin off from the 1960s Hollywood film, ran for six seasons between 1988 and 1994.

Short mini-series or television movies dealing with racial issues were also popular. In 1991 Sidney Poitier played NAACP lawyer Thurgood Marshall in a two-part account of the 1954 *Brown v. Board of Education* desegregation case. In *Mandela and De Klerk* (1997) Poitier took the role of Nelson Mandela.

Unable to compete with multi-million dollar Hollywood productions, replete with lavish special effects, makers of TV movies sought to win over audiences with films examining controversial issues like racism, alcoholism or wife battering. Television executives of the 1990s opted for a strategy of exploring adult themes to attract high viewing figures, just as Hollywood filmmakers had done in order to meet the challenge of television in the late 1940s.

In another recycling of an old image the comedy series *Benson* (1979–86) starred African American Robert Guillaume as a sharp-witted butler who gave the impression of being a modern version of Rochester. In another comedy, *Gimme a Break!* (1981–7), African American Nell Carter appeared as a portly black housekeeper in the Beulah mould.

In common with their Hollywood counterparts, television programme makers often dealt with racial issues by avoiding them altogether. Black characters thus appeared decontextualized from African American culture and society or in positive, reassuring relationships with whites in which race was not an issue. In *Diff'rent Strokes* (1978–86) two orphaned black children were cared for by a white millionaire and lived happily ever after. Similarly, in an ABC series, *Webster* (1983–7), benign white parents adopted another black orphan.

In NBC's *The 'A' Team* (1983–7), B. A. Baracus starred as the lone black character in a group of former soldiers who regularly righted wrongs while on the run after being convicted of a crime that they did not commit. Appearing as Dominique Devereaux in the glamour soap *Dynasty*, between 1984 and 1986, Diahann Carroll seemed to be as removed from black culture as she had been in her earlier incarnation as Julia.

In the NBC 'buddy-buddy' cop series *Miami Vice* (1984–9), Philip Michael Thomas, partnered with a white detective played by Don Johnson, was also cut off from African American society. In *LA Law* (1987–94), Blair Underwood played a rising black attorney, Jonathan Rollins, in an otherwise all-white law practice. Although the series did sometimes have plots with racial storylines, little was revealed about Rollins' family life. He was a black professional living in a white world.

This criticism could not be made of the Huxtable family in *The Cosby Show* (1984–92). Starring Bill Cosby and Phylicia Rashad as the parents of a black family, the sitcom was a major success for NBS. Husband Cliff, a doctor, and his wife Clair, a lawyer, were both successful in material and career terms. They were also in touch with African American culture and made sure that the children took pride in their ethnic identity. Alvin Poussaint, a black psychologist, was employed as a consultant for the show and read all scripts to ensure that there were no negative images of African American life.

An advance on earlier programmes, the show was not without weaknesses. The affluence of the family suggested that racism was no longer an issue and that affirmative action programmes were unnecessary. If black families of the 1980s lived in poverty this was a result of their own failings rather than racial barriers. The family never directly experienced racial discrimination and Cliff and Clair said nothing to indicate that they may have suffered from racism in earlier years. This was despite the fact that they had clearly come of age at the height of the civil rights movement in the 1950s and 1960s.

The most serious shortcoming of the show was its failure to reflect economic inequalities within the African American community. In real life some black Americans did experience the comfortable lifestyle enjoyed by the Huxtables but many lived in poverty. This gulf was highlighted in 1992 when the broadcast of the final episode of the show coincided with the most serious inner city race riot in years in Los Angeles.

A succession of disturbing news stories during the 1990s demonstrated that the actual state of race relations in the nation was far removed from the cosy world depicted in *The Cosby Show*. The 1992 riots in LA had been sparked off by the conclusion of the trial of a group of white policemen charged with beating a black motorist in the city, Rodney King, the previous year. A white jury acquitted the officers, even though the assault had been captured on video.

In 1991, the Senate confirmation hearings of African American Supreme Court nominee Clarence Thomas became an unlikely real-life television drama. Accused of sexual harassment by a former black co-worker, Anita Hill, Thomas claimed that the growing campaign against him was motivated by racism. He was the victim of a 'high tech lynching'. Americans tuned into the hearings on a daily basis and the controversy divided the African American community.

Between January and October 1995 the trial of O. J. Simpson attracted unprecedented media coverage and became another gripping drama for television audiences. The judge, the defence and

107

prosecution lawyers, and even witnesses and jurors, became national celebrities.

The development of cable technology in the 1990s had a major impact on television. In 1990 37 per cent of American homes had cable. By 2000 this figure had risen to 70 per cent, with viewers having more than fifty cable channels to choose from. One consequence of this competition was that programme makers, especially on the newer, smaller networks, Fox, WB and UPN, sought to target niche audiences. Fox in particular sought to air shows that were attractive to black Americans in their teens and early twenties. These included programmes like *In Living Color* (1990–3), *Martin* (1992–7) and *Living Single* (1993–8). Fast moving comedies, these shows starred, or featured guest appearances by, Hip Hop celebrities to give them added youth appeal.

At the start of the twenty-first century black and white audiences had increasingly divergent viewing patterns. Shows popular with whites, like *Seinfeld*, *Friends* and *Frazier*, barely registered in black rating lists. Conversely, programmes favoured by African Americans, such as *The Steve Harvey Show* and *The Parkers*, were largely unknown to white viewers. An ironic by-product of increased competition and new technology was that they led to increasingly segregated audiences, as had been common when television had first been introduced more than half a century earlier.

From Ragtime to Rap

When asked about the social and political content of his films, movie mogul Sam Goldwyn is reputed to have replied that pictures were for entertainment, and that if he wanted to convey a message he would send a telegram with Western Union. The weakness in this line of argument is that it presupposes that the two objectives are mutually incompatible. This is not the case. For more than a hundred years Hollywood directors have made films that both entertained and propagated their own political views.

Over several centuries American popular culture has consistently advanced negative stereotypes of African Americans, depicting them as servants, comic figures of fun or sexually predatory black brutes. Although these images have evolved, and been modified over time, they continue to be remarkably enduring.

In the early 1900s white Americans were outraged at the lifestyle of 'African Biped Beast' Jack Johnson, and relished his final demise in the boxing ring. One hundred years later Mike Tyson became a similar hate figure and white fight fans have savoured his declining fortunes. The Huck Finn complex, developed by Mark Twain in the 1880s, continued to be reprised in Hollywood productions of the 1990s.

Such representations are important. Persisting in all leading areas of popular culture – film, music, sport, radio, television – they reinforce negative stereotypes of African Americans held by their white fellow citizens. The fact that, over time, the symbolism has become more subtle and subliminal only increases the magnitude of its impact.

More disturbing, negative racial images lower the self-esteem of African Americans. In the 1954 *Brown* v. *Board of Education* case

NAACP lawyers famously introduced a series of social science studies to support their arguments for school desegregation. Presented with differing sets of dolls young African American children invariably associated qualities like intelligence, cleanliness and beauty with the white dolls whereas they perceived the black versions to be lazy, dirty and less likely to be successful. Disturbingly, the children admitted that the latter most closely approximated to their own self-image.

Born in 1942, Muhammad Ali later made the same point in his typical eloquent style. When he was growing up, he reflected, what did he see? Jesus was white, Superman was white, the President was white, the angels were white and even Santa Claus was white. 'Every year, you buy toys, and your children wind up thinking that they come from some white man with rosy cheeks.' They were brainwashed into believing that 'everything good has to come from someone white'.

During the course of the twentieth century racial images did improve, but progress was both limited and gradual. In periods of deteriorating race relations, most notably in the 1980s and 1990s, they could also regress. This reflects the fact that mainstream popular culture is essentially conservative in nature, constantly seeking the middle ground to achieve maximum audience appeal.

At the same time there are positive aspects in the ongoing relationship between African Americans and US popular culture. Rich, diverse and constantly innovative, artistic self-expression has been an enduring survival mechanism for black Americans. The African cultural survivals of ante-bellum slaves, the music of early twentieth-century Jazz and Blues artists, and the recordings of 1990s Rap performers, have helped successive generations of African Americans to bear the racial discrimination and social and economic deprivation that they encountered in their daily lives.

In the process African Americans have made a unique contribution to American life. Comprising only 12 to 13 per cent of the US population, in the twentieth century black Americans made a greater contribution to the nation's culture than any other ethnic group. From Ragtime to Rap almost all the major developments in popular music had their origins in African American society. Less encouragingly, most of the financial rewards for this creativity typically went to white financiers, business managers and crossover artists rather than black performers.

On a more positive note, recognition of the creative achievement of African Americans offers hope for the future as a way of breaking down prejudice and achieving greater racial under-standing. If in the past popular culture has all too often had the opposite effect, reinforcing negative racial attitudes, there is no scientific law that demands that this must always be the case. Shared cultural values and positive racial images can equally serve to advance race relations. To use the words of Abraham Lincoln, they have the capacity to appeal to 'the better angels of our nature'.

Further reading

There is no good holistic study on race and all the major forms of US popular culture. However, J. L. Dates and W. Barlow (eds), *Split Image: African Americans in the Mass Media* (1993) and Brian Ward (ed.), *Media, Culture and the Modern African American Freedom Struggle* (2001) are good essay collections covering a range of topics.

A good introduction to blackface minstrelsy is Robert Toll, *Blacking Up: The Minstrel Show in Nineteenth-Century America* (1974). More recent studies have tended to focus on minstrelsy as an expression of white working-class culture and social protest rather than its racial dimensions. These include Eric Lott, *Love and Theft* (1993), Annemarie Bean *et al.*, *Inside the Minstrel Mask* (1996), Dale Cockrell, *Demons of Disorder* (1997) and William J. Mahar, *Behind the Burnt Cork Mask* (1999). W. T. Lhaman, Jr., *Raising Cain* (1998) argues the case for the persistence of minstrel imagery in popular culture even in the last years of the twentieth century. On the actual culture of ante-bellum slaves, as opposed to caricatured white perceptions of it, a good introduction to what is a major topic in its own right is John Blassingame, *The Slave Community* (1972).

Sam Dennison, *Scandalize My Name* (1982) is a thoughtful study on the stereotyping of African Americans in nineteenth-century popular music. There are a number of more specialized texts on more specific aspects of musical culture. Paul Oliver, *Blues Fell This Morning* (1990) is an outstanding work demonstrating the extent to which the Blues reflected the daily realities of black life in the late nineteenth century and early years of the twentieth century. The Ken Burns extended television documentary *Jazz* (2000), now available on video, blends together thoughtful voice-over narrative with extensive, and often rare, archival footage. Geoffrey C. Ward and Ken Burns, *Jazz: A History of America's Music* (2001) is a book written to accompany the series.

On race and popular music after World War II Brian Ward, *Just My Soul Responding* (1998) is easily the best work in the field. Tracing the development of Rhythm and Blues, Rock and Roll, Soul, and Disco, Ward combines enthusiasm for his subject with scholarly insight and an encyclopaedic knowledge of record releases of the period.

There is no such definitive study on Rap, not least because of the still rapidly evolving nature of the genre. This is reflected in the best work currently available, Patricia Rose, *Black Noise* (1994) that examines the development of Rap and Hip Hop culture in the early 1990s. Unfortunately, Rose's study pre-dates the development of West Coast centred Gangsta Rap in the latter half of the decade.

There are a number of useful works looking at racial imagery in advertising and African American collectibles. These include Marilyn Kern-Foxworth, *Aunt Jemima, Uncle Ben and Rastus* (1994), Kenneth Goings, *Mammy and Uncle Mose* (1994), and Patricia A. Turner, *Ceramic Uncles and Celluloid Mammies* (1994).

On race and sport there is no good analytical narrative covering the period as a whole. John Hoberman, *Darwin's Athletes* (1997) provides some valuable insights but focuses more on the evolution of scientific and social science thought on race than the historical development of sporting activities.

In contrast there are a number of good studies on individual black sportsmen, namely William Baker, *Jesse Owens* (1986), Thomas Hauser, *Muhammad Ali* (1997), Chris Mead, *Champion Joe Louis* (1985), Randy Roberts, *Papa Jack* (1986), and Joseph Tygiel's biography of Jackie Robinson, *Baseball's Great Experiment* (1997). Gerald Suster, *Champions of the Ring* (1992) provides useful pen portraits of World Heavyweight Boxing Champions of the modern era but is written more from the perspective of a boxing devotee than a historian.

William Barlow, *Voice Over* (1999) is a reasonable study of the black experience in radio from its 1920s origins to the end of the twentieth century but is marred by a number of factual errors. Good but more specialized works include Melvin Ely, *The*

Adventures of Amos 'n' Andy (1991) and Barbara Savage, *Broadcasting Freedom* (1999).

Film has benefited from more extensive coverage providing the reader with a choice of satisfactory studies. Of the older works Daniel Leab, *From Sambo to Superspade* (1973) still provides a good introduction to the subject but has been supplanted by Donald Bogle's more modern *Toms, Coons, Mulattoes, Mammies and Bucks* (1994) that highlights the persistence of racial stereotyping in Hollywood film from its early twentieth century origins through to the 1990s.

Bogle's *Prime-Time Blues* (2001) has similarly replaced J. F. MacDonald's *Blacks and White TV* (1983) as the best one volume history on race and television. Examining the development of commercial television from its infancy in the late 1940s through to the late 1990s, Bogle's study confirms that racial imagery in mainstream popular culture continues to be a source of concern and controversy in the twenty-first century.

Select bibliography

Appiah, K. A. and H. L. Gates (eds) *Africana*, New York: Basic Books, 1999.

Baker, W. J. *Jesse Owens: An American Life*, New York: The Free Press, 1986.

Barlow, W. *Voice Over: The Making of Black Radio*, Philadelphia, Pa.: Temple University Press, 1999.

Bean, A., J. V. Hatch and B. McNamara (eds) *Inside the Minstrel Mask: Readings in Nineteenth-Century Blackface Minstrelsy*, Hanover, NH: Wesleyan University Press, 1996.

Blassingame, J. *The Slave Community*, New York: Oxford University Press 1972.

Bogle, D. *Toms, Coons, Mulattoes, Mammies and Bucks: An Interpretative History of Blacks in American Film*, New York: Continuum, 1994.

Bogle, D. *Prime-Time Blues: African Americans in Network Television*, New York: Farrar, Straus & Giroux, 2001.

Bonazzi, R. *Man in the Mirror: John Howard Griffin and the Story of Black Like Me*, New York: Orbis Books, 1997.

Boskin, J. *Sambo: The Rise and Demise of an American Jester*, Oxford: Oxford University Press, 1986.

Boyd, Todd. *Am I Black Enough For You? Popular Culture from the Hood and Beyond*, Bloomington, Ind.: Indiana University Press, 1997.

Bushart, H. L., J. R. Craig and M. Barnes, *Soldiers of God: White Supremacists and their Holy War for America*, New York: Kensington Books, 1998.

Cleaver, E. *Soul on Ice*, New York: Laurel Books, 1992.

Cockrell, D. *Demons of Disorder: Early Blackface Minstrels and their World*, Cambridge: Cambridge University Press, 1997.

Dates, J. L., and W. Barlow (eds) *Split Image: African Americans in the Mass Media*, second edition, Washington DC: Howard University Press, 1993.

Dennison, S. *Scandalize My Name: Black Imagery in American Popular Music*, New York: Garland, 1982.

Dyson, M. *Between God and Gangsta Rap: Bearing Witness to Black Culture*, Oxford: Oxford University Press, 1996.

Dyson, M. *Holler If You Hear Me: Searching for Tupac Shakur*, London: Plexis, 2001.

Edwards, H. *The Revolt of the Black Athlete*, New York: The Free Press, 1969.

Eisen, G. and D. K. Wiggins *Ethnicity and Sport in North American History and Culture*, Westport, Conn.: Greenwood Press, 1994.

Elkins, S. *Slavery: A Problem in American Institutional and Intellectual Life*, third edition, Chicago, Ill.: University of Chicago Press, 1976.

Ely, M. P. *The Adventures of Amos 'n' Andy: A Social History of an American Phenomenon*, New York: The Free Press, 1991.

Forman, M. *The 'Hood Comes First: Race, Space, and Place in Rap and Hip-Hop*, Middletown, Conn.: Wesleyan University Press, 2002.

Franklin, J. H. and A. A. Moss, *From Slavery to Freedom: A History of Negro Americans*, seventh edition, New York: McGraw Hill, 1999.

Frederickson, G. M. *The Black Image in the White Mind: The Debate on Afro-American Character and Destiny, 1817–1914*, New York: Harper Torchbooks, 1972.

George, N. *Hip Hop America*, London: Penguin Books, 1998.

Gittins, I. *Eminem*, London: Carlton Books, 2001.

Goings, K. W. *Mammy and Uncle Mose: Black Collectibles and American Stereotyping*, Bloomington, Ind.: Indiana University Press, 1994.

Graham, A. *Framing the South: Hollywood, Television and Race during the Civil Rights Struggle*, Baltimore, Md.: Johns Hopkins University Press, 2001.

Gray, H. *Watching Race: Television and the Struggle for Blackness*, Minneapolis, Minn.: University of Minnesota Press, 1995.

Gutman, H. *The Black Family in Slavery and Freedom, 1750–1925*, Oxford: Basil Blackwell, 1976.

Haley, A. *The Autobiography of Malcolm X*, London: Penguin Books, 1968.

Hauser, T. *Muhammad Ali: His Life and Times*, London: Pan Books, 1997.

Heller, P. *Bad Intentions: The Mike Tyson Story*, New York: Da Capo Press, 1995.

Hoberman, J. *Darwin's Athletes: How Sport has Damaged Black America and Preserved the Myth of Race*, Boston, Mass.: Houghton Mifflin Company, 1997.

Hoffer, R. *A Savage Business: The Comeback and Comedown of Mike Tyson*, New York: Simon & Schuster, 1998.

Hunt, D. M. *O. J. Simpson Fact and Fictions: News Rituals in the Construction of Reality*, Cambridge: Cambridge University Press, 1999.

Jhally, S. and J. Lewis, *Enlightened Racism: The Cosby Show, Audiences and the Myth of the American Dream*, Boulder, Col.: Westview Press, 1992.

Kenyatta, K. *You Forgot About Dre: The Unauthorized Biography of Dr. Dre and Eminem*, Phoenix, Ariz.: Busta Books, 2001.

Kern-Foxworth, M. *Aunt Jemima, Uncle Ben and Rastus: Blacks in Advertising, Yesterday, Today and Tomorrow*, Westport, Conn.: Greenwood Press, 1994.

Leab, D. *From Sambo to Superspade: The Black Experience in Motion Pictures*, London: Secker & Warburg, 1973.

Levine, L. *Black Culture and Black Consciousness*, Oxford: Oxford University Press, 1977.

Lhamon, W. T. *Raising Cain: Blackface Performance from Jim Crow to Hip Hop*, Cambridge, Mass.: Harvard University Press, 1998.

Ling, P. and S. Monteith (eds) *Gender in the Civil Rights Movement*, New York: Garland, 1999.

Lott, E. *Love and Theft: Blackface Minstrelsy and the American Working Class*, Oxford: Oxford University Press, 1993.

MacDonald, J. F. *Blacks and White TV: Afro-Americans in Television since 1948*, Chicago, Ill.: Nelson-Hall Publishers, 1983.

Mahar, W. J. *Behind the Burnt Cork Mask: Early Blackface Minstrelsy and Ante-bellum American Popular Culture*, Urbana, Ill.: University of Illinois Press, 1999.

Mandell, R. D. *The Nazi Olympics*, New York: Macmillan, 1971.

Manring, M. M. *Slave in a Box: The Strange Career of Aunt Jemima*, Charlottesville, Va.: University Press of Virginia, 1998.

Mead, C. *Champion Joe Louis: Black Hero in White America*, New York: Charles Scribner & Sons, 1985.

Miller, M. H. *Louis Armstrong: A Cultural Legacy*, Seattle, Wash.: University of Washington Press, 1994.

Newby, I. A. *Jim Crow's Defense: Anti-Negro Thought in America, 1900–1930*, Baton Rouge, La.: Louisiana University Press, 1965.

Oliver, P. *Blues Fell This Morning: Meaning in the Blues*, Cambridge: Cambridge University Press, 1990.

Perkins, W. E. (ed.) *Droppin' Science: Critical Essays on Rap Music and Hip Hop Culture*, Philadelphia, Pa.: Temple University Press, 1996.

Poitier, S. *The Measure of a Man*, London: Simon & Schuster, 2000.

Ridgeway, J. *Blood in the Face: The Ku Klux Klan, Aryan Nations, Nazi Skinheads and the Rise of a New White Culture*, second edition, New York: Thunder's Mouth Press, 1995.

Ro, R. *Have Gun Will Travel: The Spectacular Rise and Violent Fall of Death Row Records*, New York: Doubleday, 1998.

Roberts, R. *Papa Jack: Jack Johnson and the Era of White Hopes*, London: Robson Books, 1986.

Rose, P. *Black Noise: Rap Music and Black Culture in Contemporary America*, Hanover, NH: Wesleyan University Press, 1994.

Sailes, G. A. (ed.) *African Americans in Sport*, New Brunswick: Transaction Publishers, 1998.

Savage, B. D. *Broadcasting Freedom: Radio, War and the Politics of Race, 1938–1948*, Chapel Hill, NC: University of North Carolina Press, 1999.

Southern, E. *The Music of Black Americans: A History*, third edition, New York: W. W. Norton & Company, 1997.

Spigel, L. and M. Curtin *The Revolution Wasn't Televised: Sixties Television and Social Conflict*, New York: Routledge, 1997.

Sundquist, E. J. (ed.) *New Essays on Uncle Tom's Cabin*, Cambridge: Cambridge University Press, 1986.

Suster, G. *Champions of the Ring: The Lives and Times of Boxing's Heavyweight Heroes*, London: Robson Books, 1992.

Toll, R. C. *Blacking Up: The Minstrel Show in Nineteenth-Century America*, Oxford: Oxford University Press, 1974.

Torres, S. (ed.) *Living Color: Race and Television in the United States*, Durham, NC: Duke University Press, 1998.

Turner, P. A. *Ceramic Uncles and Celluloid Mammies: Black Images and Their Influence on Culture*, New York: Anchor Books, 1994.

Tygiel, J. *Baseball's Great Experiment: Jackie Robinson and his Legacy*, Oxford: Oxford University Press, 1997.

Van Deburg, W. L. *Slavery and Race in American Popular Culture*, Madison, Wisc.: University of Wisconsin Press, 1984.

Van Deburg, W. L. *New Day in Babylon: The Black Power Movement and American Culture, 1965–1975*, Chicago, Ill.: University of Chicago Press, 1992.

Van Deburg, W. L. *Black Camelot: African-American Culture Heroes in Their Times, 1960–1980*, Chicago, Ill.: University of Chicago Press, 1997.

Wade, W. C. *The Fiery Cross: The Ku Klux Klan in America*, New York: Simon & Schuster Inc., 1987.

Walker, J. (ed.) *Halliwell's Film and Video Guide, 2000, Fifteenth Edition*, London: HarperCollins, 1999.

Ward, B. (ed.) *Media, Culture, and the Modern African American Freedom Struggle*, Gainesville, Fla.: University Press of Florida, 2001.

Ward, B. *Just My Soul Responding: Rhythm and Blues, Black Consciousness and Race Relations*, London: UCL Press, 1998.

Ward, G. C. and K. Burns, *Jazz: A History of America's Music*, London: Pimlico, 2001.

White, S. and G. White, *Stylin': African American Expressive Culture from Its Beginnings to the Zoot Suit*, Ithaca, NY: Cornell University Press, 1998.

Wiggins, D. K. *Glory Bound: Black Athletes in White America*, New York: Syracuse University Press, 1997.

Williams, L. *Playing the Race Card: Melodrama of Black and White From Uncle Tom to O. J. Simpson*, Princeton, NJ: Princeton University Press, 2001.

Willis, S. *High Contrast: Race and Gender in Contemporary Hollywood Film*, Durham, NC: Duke University Press, 1997.

Woodard, K. *A Nation Within a Nation: Amiri Baraka (LeRoi Jones) and Black Power Politics*, Chapel Hill, NC: University of North Carolina Press, 1999.

Zook, K. B. *Color By Fox: The Fox Network and the Revolution in Black Television*, Oxford: Oxford University Press, 1999.

Television and video
Broomfield, N., Director, *Biggie and Tupac*, Optimum Releasing, 2002.
Burns, K. *Jazz*, P. S. B. Home Videos, 2000.
Celebration of the Life of Paul Robeson, London: History Now, 1998.
Riggs, M. T., Director and V. Kleiman, Producer, *Color Adjustment*, 1991.

Internet websites
CNN, <http://www.cnn.com/>.
The New York Times, <http://www.nytimes.com/>.

Index